GW01161673

The Queen's Diamond Jubilee

First Published in October 2011.

All rights reserved. No part of this publication may be reproduced, stored in a retrieval system or transmitted in any form by any means - electronic, mechanical, photocopying, recording or otherwise - without the prior permission of the publisher.

Text copyright: Rex Publications Ltd
Pictures: Press Association Images, The Royal Collection, Mary Evans Picture Library & Joe Little
Design copyright: Mpress (Media) Ltd
Editor: Joe Little

ISBN: 978-0-9570398-0-3

Published By:
Rex Publications Ltd
64 Charlotte Street London W1T 4QD
Tel: 020 7436 4006 Fax: 020 7436 3458
www.majestymagazine.com

Designed and Printed by Mpress
Unit Four, Ashton Gate, Harold Hill, Romford, RM3 8UF Telephone: 01708 379 777

Contents

CHAPTER 01:	The Early Years by Christopher Warwick	6
CHAPTER 02:	Love & Marriage by Coryne Hall	28
CHAPTER 03:	The New Reign by Ian Lloyd	50
CHAPTER 04:	The 1960s by Lucinda Gosling	72
CHAPTER 05:	The 1970s by Robert Golden	96
CHAPTER 06:	The 1980s by Ian Lloyd	120
CHAPTER 07:	The 1990s by Ingrid Seward	142
CHAPTER 08:	The 2000s by Coryne Hall	162
CHAPTER 09:	The Present Day by Christopher Warwick	180
CHAPTER 10:	Sixty Glorious Years by Joe Little	200

PICTURE INDEX: 210

FOREWORD by Ingrid Seward, Editor-in-Chief of *Majesty* magazine

WHEN QUEEN ELIZABETH II ascended the throne on 6 February 1952 she was only 25 and had two small children. In post-war Britain there was only one television channel, broadcasting in black and white to fewer than a million homes. After a sustained campaign from the BBC and Members of Parliament, the new monarch agreed to allow the coronation ceremony to be televised, resulting in a rush to buy TV sets on hire purchase.

With the slogan 'Set the people free', Sir Winston Churchill's new Conservative government promised a more prosperous Britain in which restrictions would be swept aside along with identity cards and ration books: in their place would come a new consumer age of free enterprise and a car in every family. The Queen epitomised the renewal of hope, security and optimism for the future and, above all, relief and gratitude for the greatest of luxuries – freedom and peace.

On Coronation Day, 2 June 1953, a national holiday, the government encouraged the mood of celebration; although food rationing was still in force it allowed everybody an extra 1lb of sugar, while eggs and sweets were taken off the ration list altogether. Churchill added to the atmosphere of optimism by heralding the start of the Queen's reign as the dawn of a 'New Elizabethan Age'. Over a million people came to London just to see the decorations. They were not disappointed, and the pomp and display of the Coronation surpassed anything Britain had seen since her father was crowned in 1937.

The dictionary definition of the word 'jubilee' is 'an occasion of rejoicing and festivity'. This book is *Majesty*'s celebration of Queen Elizabeth II's remarkable 60-year reign during which the world has changed beyond all recognition. On her 21st birthday, Princess Elizabeth vowed publicly that she viewed her life as one of service; she believed that once crowned and anointed only death could break her from the oath she swore at her coronation.

Since those austere days of the 1950s, the Queen has witnessed wars and death and tragedies but never once has she allowed her personal problems or views to interfere with duty. But no ship of state, however well constructed, is entirely waterproof, and the breakdown of the marriage of the Prince and Princess of Wales blew a jagged gash in the monarchy's plating. When Diana died, the Queen, possibly for the first time in her reign, was confronted with a situation beyond her control and for one tumultuous, clamorous week the outpourings of public anger against the Crown threatened to overwhelm the House of Windsor.

The Queen may not like some of the changes that have been forced upon her during her reign, but she has accepted them. Her routine, however, is still unswerving: Christmas at Sandringham; Easter at Windsor and the summer at Balmoral. Although she might go riding or work her dogs during her breaks, she never stops completely and there are regular meetings with her private secretaries and the official boxes to deal with. She very seldom travels abroad except on official duty and with the loss of the Royal Yacht *Britannia* in 1997, which provided her with a home away from home, overseas tours have become more demanding, not less. The Queen is, as always, uncomplaining, but she is not superhuman and obviously must find such trips exhausting. She has no intention of giving up, however, and although Prince Philip has said he will cut down on his official duties, he does not appear to be doing so as he feels his place is at her side, as it has been for the last 64 years.

The Diamond Jubilee will be an opportunity for both British and overseas subjects to celebrate with Her Majesty her long and illustrious reign and give thanks to her for the sacrifices she has made in the name of our country and the Commonwealth.

Ingrid Seward

6 The Queen's Diamond Jubilee

CHAPTER 1

The Early Years

by CHRISTOPHER WARWICK

THE SPRING OF 1926 was a time of nationwide alarm, affecting every level of society, from the poorest worker to the King himself. Precipitated by the withdrawal of the government's subsidy to the coal industry and a bitter dispute between coal miners and mine owners over pay cuts and increased working hours, the entire country was brought to a standstill by the first ever General Strike in British history.

It was against this political backdrop – and, so far as public interest was concerned, in direct contrast to it – that the Duke and Duchess of York's first child was born, nearly three years to the day since Lady Elizabeth Bowes Lyon had married Prince Albert, Duke of York, the second of King George V and Queen Mary's five surviving children. Without a permanent London home of their own, Elizabeth and 'Bertie', as the Duke was known to his family, moved into number 17 Bruton Street, in the heart of Mayfair. It was the London home of the Duchess of York's parents, the Earl and Countess of Strathmore, who were, ironically, among England's most prominent coal-mine owners. The house no longer exists; today, the site is occupied by an unsympathetic building, partly occupied by an upmarket Chinese restaurant.

THE EARLY YEARS

In April 1926, however, 17 Bruton Street and the event taking place there was the focus of attention not only of an eager nation but also of an equally eager press, who may, at least in part, have regarded it as a brief distraction to the fermenting mood of industrial unrest.

On a night of 'evil April drizzle', as a contemporary report described it, the 25-year-old Duchess of York endured a difficult labour. As the hours passed, concern increased when it became clear that the unborn baby was in the breech position. Some time after midnight, the attendant gynaecologists decided to take what was later described as 'a certain line of treatment', decorous code for what was, in fact, birth by Caesarean section.

A few hours later, it was officially announced to the world that 'Her Royal Highness the Duchess of York was safely delivered of a Princess at 2.40am this morning, Wednesday, 21st April'; the Court Circular formally recorded that the King and Queen, who were in residence at Windsor, 'received with great pleasure the news that the Duchess of York gave birth to a daughter this morning'.

At her christening in the private chapel at Buckingham Palace on 29 May, by the Archbishop of Canterbury, Cosmo Gordon Lang, the baby Princess cried throughout and had eventually to be pacified with a bottle of dill water. She was dressed in the robe of cream satin and Honiton lace that had been worn by eight of Queen Victoria's nine children and by nearly every royal baby until quite recently. Baptised with water from the River Jordan, the Princess received the names Elizabeth Alexandra Mary, in honour of her mother, her late great-grandmother Queen Alexandra, who had died just six months before, and her grandmother, Queen Mary.

At the time of her birth, Princess Elizabeth of York was third in line to the throne, immediately after her father and his elder brother, the Prince of Wales. Behind her were her uncles Henry (later Duke of Gloucester) and George (afterwards Duke of Kent), and her aunt Mary (the future Princess Royal), who each moved down a notch. In time, it was fully expected that the young Princess and her father would similarly be displaced when the Prince of Wales – despite his penchant for affairs with other men's wives – married and had children of his own.

In the 1920s and early 1930s, the idea that Princess Elizabeth might become queen entered nobody's head. In fact, for almost the first decade of their marriage, the Duke and Duchess of York had no reason to believe that the tone and nature of their lives would alter very much, if at all, in the future.

8 The Queen's Diamond Jubilee

CHAPTER 1

The Queen's Diamond Jubilee 9

THE EARLY YEARS

CHAPTER 1

It was also in 1926 that the Yorks took a lease on their first permanent London residence. Though destroyed when it took a direct hit from a German bomb during the Second World War – the InterContinental Hotel now stands on the site – 145 Piccadilly was an elegant terraced townhouse, four doors along from Apsley House, the Duke of Wellington's more famous mansion at Hyde Park Corner.

When the infant Princess was brought to her new home, she was entrusted to the care of Clara Cooper Knight, known as Allah (pronounced Ah-la), an old-fashioned, no-nonsense nanny, who was greatly loved by all her charges, including the baby's own mother.

With the birth of Princess Elizabeth – or 'Lilibet' as she called herself during early attempts to pronounce her first name – Allah Knight moved into the top floor of No. 145 with its sunlit day nursery and pink and fawn night nursery, both of which opened on to a circular landing beneath a large glass dome. It was here that Lilibet 'stabled' as many as 30 toy horses. It has been said that her lifelong passion for horses first seriously began when her father took Naseby Hall in Northamptonshire for the hunting season in 1928. Be that as it may, her earliest impressions were almost certainly formed when she was taken for a daily ride along Rotten Row, the famous equestrian thoroughfare in Hyde Park, in a landau sent from the Royal Mews.

She would also have seen horses drawing carts and carriages from the nursery suite, the front windows of which overlooked Piccadilly and the northwest corner of Green Park in one direction and diagonally across Wellington Arch and Hyde Park Corner to St George's Hospital (now the five-star Lanesborough Hotel) in the other.

Playing at horses was also by far and away the best sort of game, whether it was tying a skipping rope round the bed knobs and driving an imaginary team around an imaginary park or, as an astonished Archbishop of Canterbury discovered on one occasion, getting 'Grandpa', King George V, down on all fours to lead him around the room by his beard. Running a 'horse-market', another favourite, involved all the toy horses ranged round the stairwell. Of varying sizes and descriptions, with or without wheels, but all with saddles and bridles, each one of them, as Princess Margaret would recall, 'had to be groomed, fed and watered all day!'

Right from the start, public interest in the Yorks' first-born extended far beyond Great Britain. In 1927, when her parents made a long official visit to Australia and New Zealand, 'Princess Betty' as 'the World's Best Known Baby' was called, was the object of intense curiosity. 'Wherever we go cheers are given for her as well & the children write to us about her,' the Duke of York told his mother, Queen Mary.

The 'Lilibet' phenomenon was global. Her photograph was to be found on the front pages of newspapers and magazines, while her outfits and their particular shades of yellow or blue, were slavishly copied and enterprising publishers produced cut-out paper dolls, complete with wardrobe. Throughout the Empire, the United States and in Europe, demand for Lilibet lookalikes mushroomed.

The Queen's Diamond Jubilee 11

THE EARLY YEARS

CHAPTER 1

By the time the Duchess of York was expecting her second child, a second and far greater calamity than the General Strike of 1926 had started to unfold. The earliest rumblings of the Great Depression, which had begun in America in August 1929 and resulted in the Wall Street Crash two months later, had profound repercussions at home, with a significant decline in industrial output and escalating unemployment affecting those who were already hardest hit in the coal mines, iron foundries and shipyards of northeast England, Scotland and Wales.

In the same way that Princess Elizabeth's birth had occurred at a time of widespread anxiety, so her only sibling Princess Margaret (or Margaret Rose as she was christened 10 weeks after her birth at Glamis Castle on 21 August 1930) made her appearance, into a world struggling to cope in far graver circumstances.

With the arrival of their second daughter, the Yorks were regarded as the archetypal 'ideal' family. Certainly, Elizabeth and Margaret, who would always be extremely close to one another despite the fact that in character and temperament they were as different as chalk and cheese (the elder more reserved, though down to earth and self-assured, the younger more precocious, less confident but more extrovert) continued to be a source of endless fascination and, indeed, adoration, to a public whose appetite was insatiable.

The Queen's Diamond Jubilee 13

THE EARLY YEARS

Without a garden of their own, the Princesses – who, in the schoolroom or at play, at a smart event, a party or out riding, were always dressed alike – played their games in Hamilton Gardens, the private communal garden that ran behind the houses on their part of Piccadilly. In the centre stood a statue of Lord Byron, which invariably served as 'home base' in the sisters' races and games of tag and hide-and-seek. There were other games, too, which involved climbing in and out of the bushes as pirates, or cowboys and indians and while playing a variation of 'Sardines'.

One of the misconceptions created by the Princesses' governess Marion Crawford, or 'Crawfie' as she was called, was that Elizabeth and Margaret lived in isolation from other children. While it is certainly true that their friends were drawn from a pretty select group, they nevertheless saw a good deal of their favourite cousin Margaret Elphinstone (who always got roped into playing horses – be they carthorses, racehorses or circus horses); of Lady Mary Cambridge, the daughter of the Marquess and Marchioness of Cambridge; of Elizabeth Cavendish, who was the daughter of the 10th Duke of Devonshire; and Patrick Plunket, son of the 6th Baron Plunket, who would one day become Deputy Master of the Household when Lilibet became Queen. There were also friendships with the children of courtiers and neighbours, one of whom, Nicky Beaumont, younger son of Lord Allendale, lived right next door at 144 Piccadilly.

Yet, even when they were at play on the lawns and gravel paths of Hamilton Gardens, the Princesses, in what at times must have seemed like a zoo-like enclosure, were rarely free from the attentions of strangers, who all too often gathered at the open railings to watch them.

Privacy was assured, however, in the idyllic setting of Royal Lodge, located at the heart of 90 secluded acres in the centre of Windsor Great Park. This is where, surrounded by its own carefully manicured garden, a remarkable thatched cottage was erected. It is two-thirds natural size, with electric light, hot running water, a functioning kitchen and furniture that had been made to scale.

CHAPTER 1

Given to Princess Elizabeth by the people of Wales for her sixth birthday in 1932, it also sought, or so it has been claimed, 'to connect the lives of the little Princess and her baby sister to those of thousands of children who inhabited real cottages'. Whether or not either Princess was ever consciously aware of this, both were reported to enjoy dusting, cleaning and tidying up, revelling in the fantasy of the miniature world that *Y Bwthyn Bach* – the Little House, as it is called – provided.

In common with the daughters of many aristocratic houses at that time, Princess Elizabeth and her sister were educated privately at home, chiefly by their governess, who provided them with what today is regarded as a basic education. The Duchess of York herself took them for Bible reading. In addition to the 'Three Rs', they had lessons in singing, dancing, music and drawing, and there were also occasional 'educational visits' to places of interest, including the Tower of London, museums and art galleries. On one occasion, they even had the novel experience of journeying on the Underground from Green Park to Tottenham Court Road, where they made an unofficial visit to the YWCA.

Yet, one inescapable aspect of the Princesses' lives was learned through experience. This was the pomp and pageantry of state and ceremonial royal occasions. Before she was 10, Princess Elizabeth would be present at three such events: the celebration of the Silver Jubilee of her grandparents' reign in 1935, and the weddings, at which she was a bridesmaid, of her uncles George of Kent and Henry of Gloucester.

The Queen's Diamond Jubilee 15

THE EARLY YEARS

There was still no sign, however, of the one wedding the country keenly awaited, that of the Prince of Wales. When, all too soon, it became an issue, it would ultimately result in one of the shortest reigns in British royal history.

In January 1936, Princess Elizabeth's beloved Grandpa, George V, died at Sandringham and the Prince of Wales ascended the throne as King Edward VIII. The events that separated the new King's accession on 20 January and his abdication on 11 December, and the reason for it – his determination to marry the American divorcee Wallis Warfield Simpson – devastated his family, sent shockwaves around the world and invested Princess Elizabeth's traumatised father, who became King George VI, with a burden of responsibility for which he was neither trained nor prepared. The Abdication also focused attention on Princess Elizabeth herself in a way that had never seriously been imagined possible; as heiress presumptive, as she now became, she stood but a heartbeat away from becoming queen.

With the York family's unexpected and even unwanted change of fortune, there also came a not altogether welcome change of address. Marion Crawford recalled, 'When I broke the news to Margaret and Lilibet that they were going to live in Buckingham Palace, they looked at me in horror. "What!" Lilibet exclaimed. "You mean for ever?"'

George VI referred to himself, his wife and their daughters as 'Us Four'. They were, as the late Princess Alice, Countess of Athlone put it, a 'small, absolutely united circle'. It was that image of loving intimacy, the reality of which was unique within British royal families, that played its part in helping to stabilise what the King, in the immediate aftermath of the Abdication, referred to as 'this rocking throne'. It also contributed very significantly to the success of George VI's reign.

As heiress presumptive, 11-year-old Princess Elizabeth's first and grandest state occasion – in a sense, a rite of passage – was the Coronation of her parents at Westminster Abbey. Writing of the ceremony in a commemorative essay, the title page of which read 'The Coronation 12th May, 1937. To Mummy and Papa In Memory of Their Coronation From Lilibet By Herself', the Princess said, 'I thought it all very, very wonderful and I expect the Abbey did, too. The arches and beams at the top were covered with a sort of haze of wonder as Papa was crowned, at least I thought so. When Mummy was crowned and all the peeresses put on their coronets it looked wonderful to see arms and coronets hovering in the air and then the arms disappear as if by magic.'

While some aspects of Elizabeth's life would remain unaltered, as heiress presumptive (and later as queen) she would always be set apart from all but a select few of her contemporaries. It was, of course, the nature of her position. And it was because of her position and what it represented in the long term, that it was decided she should have tuition in constitutional history.

As one observer remarked, Crawfie 'had been employed to help the Princesses become lady-like, not monarchical'. The role of tutor to Elizabeth, who took lessons with him twice a week, fell to Sir Henry Marten, the Vice-Provost of Eton, just across the Thames from Windsor Castle and a few miles from Royal Lodge.

THE EARLY YEARS

18 The Queen's Diamond Jubilee

At the time of Princess Elizabeth's birth, there was justifiable disillusionment that Britain had not become the 'land fit for heroes' that had been promised in the aftermath of the Great War. It had been one of the subsidiary causes of the General Strike. Yet, just 20 years after the guns had fallen silent in 1918, the world stood poised on the brink of another deadly conflagration, with Adolf Hitler's Germany once again the aggressor. In July 1939, as the proverbial war clouds gathered, George VI paid a visit to the Royal Naval College at Dartmouth. The Queen and the Princesses were with him as he disembarked from the then Royal Yacht *Victoria and Albert*.

Although their paths had crossed at the wedding of Prince George, Duke of Kent with Princess Marina of Greece in 1934, and very probably on other family occasions too, this is when, as popular history would have it, Elizabeth first met her future husband: Prince Philip of Greece and Denmark, the only son of Prince Andrew of Greece and Princess Alice of Battenberg, a great-granddaughter of Queen Victoria. Although it isn't likely that the 18-year-old Philip, then a promising special entry cadet at Dartmouth with a naval career ahead of him, felt the same way about his distant cousin, who was then only 13 and still in white socks, she took what has been described as 'a friendly and romantic interest' in him. From then on, they wrote to one another on a regular basis and over the next few years often met. It was only a matter of time before they fell in love.

Meanwhile, though the prospect of war loomed ever closer, King George, Queen Elizabeth and the Princesses travelled up to Balmoral as usual that August for their summer holiday. But when, only three weeks later, news was received that Germany and Russia had entered into a pact and that in consequence Parliament had been recalled, the King returned immediately to London. The Queen joined him five days later. Their daughters, however, were to remain in Scotland, at Birkhall on the royal estate. War was declared on 3 September, and though Elizabeth and Margaret, together with their cousin Margaret Elphinstone, were safe and far removed from danger, the reality of war still penetrated their tranquil surroundings: in mid-October, it was announced that the battleship *Royal Oak* had been torpedoed by a German U-boat that had slipped through the defences of the northern naval base at Scapa Flow, with the loss of over 800 lives. Angrily jumping up from her chair, Princess Elizabeth exclaimed, 'It can't be! All those nice sailors.'

THE EARLY YEARS

Despite the fact that it was close to one of the stretches of North Sea coast that was thought most likely to be targeted in the event of enemy invasion, the Princesses were delighted to be told that Christmas that year would be spent as usual at Sandringham. And it was there that they stayed until February 1940, when they returned to Royal Lodge, Windsor, its distinctive pink walls now repainted in the murky shades of camouflage to protect it from air attack. Three months later, however, on 12 May, which also happened to be the third anniversary of their parents' coronation, the Queen instructed Marion Crawford that, for their greater safety, she was to take Elizabeth and Margaret to Windsor Castle, 'at least for the rest of the week'. As it turned out, they were to remain there for the next five years, under the protection of a 300-strong company of Grenadier Guards. The reason for their move was that only two days before, on 10 May, having already invaded Denmark and Norway, Hitler had launched a massive ground and air attack on Holland, Belgium and Luxembourg.

CHAPTER 1

The Queen's Diamond Jubilee 21

THE EARLY YEARS

Throughout the war, when they were not travelling the length and breadth of the country on morale-boosting visits, the King and Queen commuted on a daily basis by armoured car from Windsor to London. The Princesses, however, did not always see as much of their parents as they would have liked and it was the theme of separation that was emphasised in the first ever BBC radio broadcast Princess Elizabeth made.

Speaking from Windsor Castle, in October 1940, she addressed all those children who had had to leave their city homes and who, unlike the Princesses themselves, were experiencing evacuation to unfamiliar places, most often entrusted to the care of complete strangers. 'Thousands of you in this country have had to leave your homes and be separated from your father and mother,' she said, reading from the script that she had carefully rehearsed. 'My sister Margaret Rose and I feel so much for you, as we know from experience what it means to be away from those we love most of all...'

Life at Windsor Castle for the two Princesses was governed by the same austere measures that applied to the rest of the population. In the castle's dimly-lit, unheated rooms, food rationing, like the regulation level of bathwater, was strictly observed. Gas masks were always at hand and at night when the air raid sirens sounded – enemy aircraft 'always seemed to come over when we had just got to sleep,' Princess Margaret recalled – they were got up, dressed in their siren suits, and with small suitcases containing their most valued possessions, were taken down into what seemed like the bowels of the earth, to the concrete shelter that was built beneath the Queen's Tower.

During the day, while the parkland surrounding Windsor Castle was turned over to food production or used as pasture for sheep and cattle, Elizabeth and Margaret 'dug for victory' in the vegetable gardens they cultivated, continued their activities in the Guides and Sea Rangers, to which both belonged, and took leading roles in Christmas pantomimes – *Cinderella, The Sleeping Beauty, Aladdin* and *Old Mother Red Riding Boots* – that were staged in the Waterloo Chamber. Like other families, they grieved at the loss of close relations, including their uncle George of Kent, who in August 1942 was killed in an air crash while on active service with the RAF.

THE EARLY YEARS

CHAPTER 1

According to Marion Crawford, both Princesses 'were always immensely interested in airmen', with fighter pilots of the RAF being regarded as special heroes. Their admiration, however, also extended to the American pilots and GIs they met. At that time, on Smith's Lawn in Windsor Great Park, which had once been where Edward VIII landed his private aircraft and which is today more famous as the home of the Guards Polo Club, the United States Air Force established a base for 14 Dakota aircraft and 25 officers, put up in tented accommodation.

When introduced to King's George VI's daughters, the Americans' invariable opening line was: 'I have a little girl at home just your age'. Knowing what to expect, both Princesses had to fight to suppress their giggles, though on one occasion Margaret whispered to her governess, 'the children there must be in America, all our age. Billions of them!'

Princess Elizabeth, who had been agitating to be allowed to do so, finally enlisted with the Transport Division of the Auxiliary Territorial Service (ATS) in early 1945. As Number 230873 Second Subaltern Elizabeth Windsor, she reported for training at Aldershot, where she learned how to strip and service an engine, and became proficient in vehicle maintenance; leading her mother to say on one occasion, 'We had spark plugs all through dinner.'

The Queen's Diamond Jubilee 25

THE EARLY YEARS

By this time there was already confident talk within circles close to the royal family, as well as speculation in the foreign press, about a marriage between Princess Elizabeth and Prince Philip. Though they were by now unmistakably in love, the King told his mother that both he and the Queen felt Elizabeth, who was then only 18, was too young for marriage. Nevertheless, the Princess very clearly knew her own mind and her parents were left in little doubt about where she was heading. Her conversations were always full of 'Philip says...' or 'Philip thinks...' When the war was finally over, however, and the Princess was that much older, views had changed.

Yet, before anything else, there came a strenuous three-month tour of South Africa, which the royal family undertook in early 1947. It was there, in April, that Princess Elizabeth celebrated her 21st birthday. From Cape Town, three days before the royal family set sail on their homeward voyage, she broadcast a message to the peoples of the Empire.

'There is a motto,' she began, 'which has been borne by many of my ancestors – a noble motto, "I swear". Those words were an inspiration to many bygone heirs to the throne when they made their knightly dedication as they came to manhood. I cannot do quite as they did, but... I can make my solemn act of dedication now.'

In what is almost certainly the most memorable of the speeches she has ever made, the Princess continued, 'I declare before you all that my whole life, whether it be long or short, shall be devoted to your service and the service of our great Imperial Commonwealth to which we all belong.'

During the royal family's absence, a notice appeared in *The London Gazette*, the most important official journal in which certain statutory notices have to be published, to the effect that HRH Prince Philip of Greece and Denmark had become a naturalised British subject. Now known simply as 'Lieutenant Philip Mountbatten, RN', he had dispensed with his royal titles, his Greek nationality and ostensible surnames of Schleswig-Holstein-Sonderburg-Glücksburg. His newly adopted last name was that of his vastly ambitious and dynastically astute 'Uncle Dickie', otherwise Earl Mountbatten of Burma, who had done everything within his power to promote and encourage his nephew's marriage to England's future queen.

On 10 July, Elizabeth and Philip's engagement was formally announced by King George VI and Queen Elizabeth, and enthusiastically welcomed by press and public alike, not least because the young Princess's popularity had never been greater. Posing for photographs the following day, Elizabeth proudly displayed her specially-designed engagement ring, made up of 11 diamonds, including a central solitaire of three carats that had once been part of a tiara owned by Philip's mother.

In its leader of 11 July 1947, *The Daily Express* was of the opinion that '...the betrothal of Princess Elizabeth and Lieutenant Mountbatten heightens the ordinary man's sense of history [and] enables him to project the past into the future and to see the rich pattern of events'.

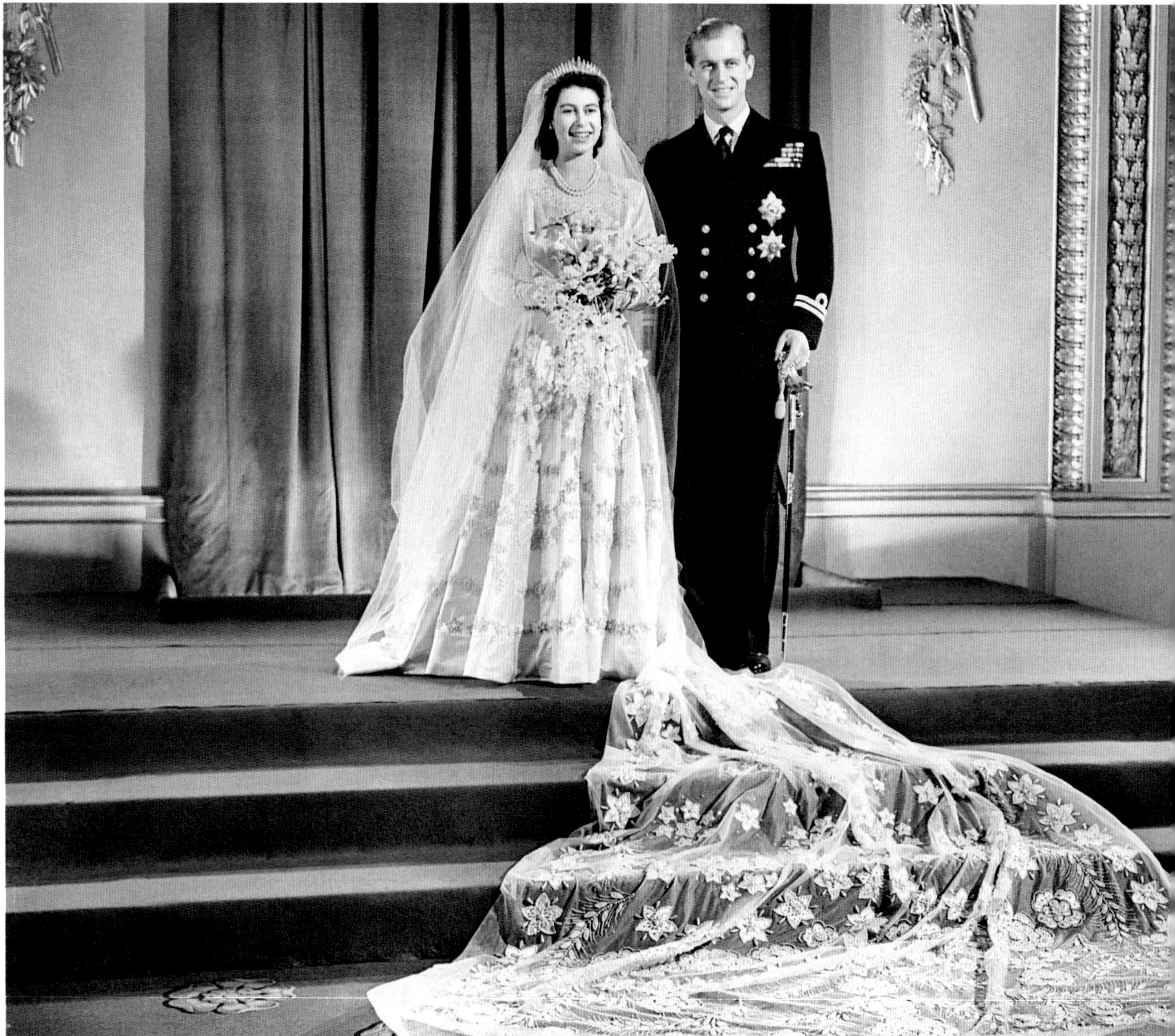

CHAPTER 2

Love & Marriage

by CORYNE HALL

THE MORNING OF 20 November 1947 was dull and cloudy but nothing could dim Princess Elizabeth's spirits on her wedding day.

Norman Hartnell had designed a romantic wedding gown based on a Botticelli painting. Made from ivory silk satin and decorated with more than 10,000 pearls forming garlands of star flowers, wheat ears and the white rose of York, it had an embroidered train 15ft long. Like other post-war brides, the Princess had collected clothing coupons for her wedding dress, although the allowance had been supplemented by material previously purchased by both the Queen and Queen Mary.

It took an hour and a quarter to dress the bride but there were some last-minute panics as mishaps occurred. Her diamond fringe tiara snapped and had to be hastily repaired, and the bouquet of white orchids made by the Worshipful Company of Gardeners disappeared but was finally found by a footman in a cupboard. The Princess decided to wear one of her parents' wedding gifts, a double string of pearls, so her Private Secretary Jock Colville had to fight his way on foot through the crowds to retrieve it from a display of wedding presents at St James's Palace.

Finally King George VI and his elder daughter left for Westminster Abbey in the Irish State Coach. Although in a nod to austerity street decorations were few, the wedding was described by Winston Churchill as 'a flash of colour on the hard road we have to travel'.

Meanwhile Philip had arrived at the abbey with his best man, his cousin David, the Marquess of Milford Haven, who looked after the wedding ring fashioned from a nugget of Welsh gold from the Clogau St David's Mine in Snowdonia. Although the bridegroom appeared on the order of service as Lieutenant Philip Mountbatten R.N., that morning the King made him Duke of Edinburgh, Earl of Merioneth and Baron Greenwich.

LOVE & MARRIAGE

CHAPTER 2

The large turnout of royalty included five kings, five queens and several European princes and princesses. Philip's widowed mother Princess Alice of Greece was present but his sisters, all married to Germans, were not invited. Sensibilities were still too strong after the war. The Duke of Windsor was also not invited as the wounds caused by his abdication were still too raw.

Among the eight bridesmaids were Princess Margaret, Princess Alexandra of Kent and Lady Pamela Mountbatten, while five-year-old Prince Michael of Kent and Prince William of Gloucester were pageboys. Elizabeth promised to 'obey' her husband, and the Archbishop of York said in his address that the ceremony was essentially the same as it would be for any cottager in a remote village.

Unlike other weddings it was broadcast by radio in 42 languages and, although television cameras were not permitted to film the service, newsreels around the world showed film of the bridal party leaving the abbey.

The Duke and Duchess of Edinburgh returned to Buckingham Palace escorted by the Household Cavalry, resplendent in full ceremonial dress for the first time in eight years. At the wedding breakfast bunches of white Balmoral heather decorated the tables and the speeches were kept short at the King's request. With rationing still in force, ingredients for the 9ft-high official wedding cake, made by McVitie and Price, had been sent as gifts from overseas.

The Queen's Diamond Jubilee 31

LOVE & MARRIAGE

As dusk fell the couple drove from the palace in an open carriage pursued by laughing guests showering them with confetti. Tucked under the rugs amongst the hot water bottles was Elizabeth's corgi Susan. When the carriage reached Waterloo Station, the dog stole the show by emerging first in a shower of paper petals.

The first part of the honeymoon was spent at Broadlands, the Hampshire home of Philip's uncle, Lord Mountbatten. A few photographers were allowed into the grounds to take pictures of the couple and sightseers hovered everywhere hoping for the slightest glimpse of the famous newlyweds. When they went to Sunday morning service at Romsey Abbey people used chairs, ladders or even tombstones to climb up and peer through the windows for a better view. After a few days the couple left for Birkhall in Scotland, where amid the winter snow they finally found solitude.

Work on Clarence House, their London residence, had not yet been completed so, like many newly married couples at the time, they had no home of their own. The Princess's great-aunt, Princess Alice, Countess of Athlone, and her husband the Earl of Athlone, who were absent overseas, lent them Clock House at Kensington Palace for a few weeks but obviously when they returned home the Edinburghs had to move out.

Even Sunninghill Park, the country home between Ascot and Windsor Great Park designated for them by the King, had burnt down before they could occupy it. As Philip was working at the Admiralty in London they moved into a suite at Buckingham Palace. With the Princess was her devoted dresser Bobo MacDonald, who still called her 'Lilibet'; the Duke had his valet, John Dean. Every day at 4.30pm the Princess stood at her window, waiting for her husband to come through the palace gates.

CHAPTER 2

The Queen's Diamond Jubilee 33

LOVE & MARRIAGE

With the help of her ladies-in-waiting the Princess carried out official duties and attended to her correspondence. In the early months she depended on her mother for advice or approval but gradually became more self-reliant. Elizabeth was basically shy and often outshone by the superb social skills of her mother and sister, but Philip, who suggested phrasing for her speeches and took the lead in any potentially awkward situations, supported her. The King was still giving her lessons in statecraft and she had access to Foreign Office telegrams, which arrived in specially-made red boxes.

Within four months of her wedding the Princess discovered she was pregnant. Despite this, in May 1948 the Duke and Duchess of Edinburgh undertook their first official visit abroad, a four-day trip to Paris. Against the background of the Cold War, with communism now the main enemy, the trip was engineered to stress Anglo-French solidarity. The visit followed a pattern that would later become familiar – the opening of the exhibition *Eight Centuries of British Life in Paris*, a reception to meet prominent Parisian dignitaries and a dinner at the British Embassy. There was one lighter moment for the Princess when, after church on Sunday, they went to the races at Longchamp. When Elizabeth visited Versailles and Fontainebleau, or sparkled in rubies and diamonds at the Opéra, she impressed everyone with her beauty and her excellent French accent.

Nobody could have guessed that the pregnant Princess was at times extremely unwell and suffering from the intense heat. The glamorous couple took the French capital by storm and by the time they left cries of '*Vive la Princesse*' were heard everywhere.

Princess Elizabeth gave birth to a son at Buckingham Palace at 9.14pm on 14 November 1948. The happy news was greeted with gun salutes, bells, bonfires and fountains running 'blue for a boy' all week. Letters Patent had been hastily issued to give the child 'the style, title or attribute of Royal Highness and the titular dignity of Prince or Princess', and the King abolished the centuries-old practice of the Home Secretary being in attendance during the royal birth.

CHAPTER 2

The Queen's Diamond Jubilee 35

LOVE & MARRIAGE

Prince Charles Philip Arthur George was christened in the Music Room at Buckingham Palace (the chapel having been bombed during the war) on 15 December. The name 'Charles' caused some surprise in royal circles because of its association with the unlucky Stuarts, but the couple had chosen the name simply because they liked it. 'Don't you think he is quite adorable?' the Princess wrote to a friend. 'I still can't believe he is really mine but perhaps that happens to new parents. Anyway, this particular boy's parents couldn't be more proud of him.'

Although she nursed him herself, Helen Lightbody, a former nanny to the Duke and Duchess of Gloucester's sons, was engaged as nanny, with Mabel Anderson as nurserymaid. There was no new pram. Princess Elizabeth's old one was refurbished for her first-born.

Underlying the joy of motherhood was concern for her father. The 54-year-old King had been suffering from cramp in his legs, which developed into arteriosclerosis. It was feared that his right leg might have to be amputated, although thankfully this did not prove necessary. Reluctantly he was forced to postpone a planned tour of Australia and New Zealand. Early in March 1949 surgeons performed a lumbar sympathectomy successfully at Buckingham Palace but at the Birthday Parade that June the monarch rode in a carriage. Princess Elizabeth, in the uniform of a Colonel of the Grenadier Guards, rode side-saddle, playing an active part in the ceremony for the first time. Two years later, in her father's absence, there would be another first when she took the salute.

There were other changes that would affect her life. In 1949 India became a republic within the Commonwealth. In future, only the United Kingdom and the old dominions, now to be known as 'realms', would swear allegiance to King George VI.

In May 1949 Elizabeth and Philip finally moved into Clarence House. The Duke of Edinburgh, who had not experienced a settled home life since he was 10 years old, had thrown himself into the project with gusto, installing many modern labour-saving devices. For a country home they rented Windlesham Moor, a five-bedroomed, four reception-roomed house within easy reach of Windsor. On Sundays they drove over to Royal Lodge to join the King and Queen for Matins in the private chapel in the grounds.

CHAPTER 2

The Queen's Diamond Jubilee 37

LOVE & MARRIAGE

Philip still longed to go back to sea. In the autumn his wish was granted when he was appointed first lieutenant of HMS *Chequers*, part of the Mediterranean Fleet based on the tiny island of Malta. Also there were Earl and Countess Mountbatten of Burma, who were living at Villa Guardamangia in Valletta while the Earl was serving as Flag Officer of the First Cruiser Squadron.

After celebrating their son's first birthday Elizabeth flew out to join her husband for their second wedding anniversary. She spent a few dutiful nights at the governor's residence before moving into Villa Guardamangia. Prince Charles was left at home in the care of his grandparents and nanny. Although the Princess received regular reports on his progress, she did not see her son again for five weeks.

Between Christmas 1949 and the summer of 1951 Princess Elizabeth experienced something approaching normal married life while staying in Malta. She went shopping (although shopkeepers reported that she was slow in handling money), visited the hairdresser and dined and danced with Philip at the Hotel Phoenicia. Unlike the other officers' wives, she had an ever-present policeman and a lady-in-waiting (often Pamela Mountbatten) and was addressed as 'Ma'am'. Ever dutiful, she occasionally visited a school or hospital but the real eye-opener was the sight of the very poor living in caves.

After three months back in England, she returned to Malta at the end of March. In the warm Mediterranean weather she and Philip went swimming, enjoyed picnics and took small boats out to explore the island's beaches and coves. Sometimes they sailed over to the neighbouring island of Gozo. Elizabeth particularly enjoyed the polo matches, a sport at which the Duke was rapidly becoming accomplished, encouraged by his uncle Dickie. On her 24th birthday Mountbatten's flag captain organised a group of young officers into an impromptu choir to sing *Happy Birthday* over the telephone, followed by a skirl of bagpipes. The Princess was delighted.

LOVE & MARRIAGE

She returned to Clarence House in May to await the birth of her second child, due in the summer. After a separation of nearly three months Philip arrived home on leave in time for the birth of Princess Anne Elizabeth Alice Louise on 15 August. Among Elizabeth's first visitors was her mother-in-law Princess Alice of Greece, who arrived at Clarence House dressed in her grey nun's habit.

Philip returned to Malta after his daughter's birth to take up his first command, the frigate HMS *Magpie*. In December, when she had finished nursing her daughter, Elizabeth joined him on the island. Charles and Anne remained with their grandparents and spent Christmas at Sandringham, from where their mother received regular progress reports.

Elizabeth has since been criticised for the amount of time she spent away from her children in these early years but in those days it was customary for royal children to be handed over to the care of nannies; their parents saw them for just a few hours a day. The Princess usually saw Charles and Anne for 30 minutes in the morning and again in the evening, while they were bathed and put to bed. Although Elizabeth was a mother she was also heiress presumptive to the throne. As the King's health deteriorated so her royal duties increased and time with her children had to be rationed.

From Malta, HMS *Magpie* was sent on several ceremonial exercises to fly the British flag in Mediterranean ports. In December 1950 it was the turn of Philip's birthplace, Greece, which he was anxious to show to his wife. Elizabeth travelled on HMS *Surprise*, as the commander-in-chief decided there was no suitable accommodation for her aboard *Magpie*.

This arrangement caused a lively exchange of signals between the vessels. *Surprise* to *Magpie*: 'Princess full of beans.' *Magpie* to *Surprise*: 'Is that the best you can give her for breakfast?'

After a state drive through Athens with King Paul and Queen Frederica, Philip's cousins, Princess Elizabeth inspected a guard of honour of Evzones, in their traditional red toques, embroidered tunics and white pleated kilts. They later saw the floodlit Parthenon and attended a state dinner at the palace. There were also some more informal moments. Lady Norton, the British

40 The Queen's Diamond Jubilee

ambassador's wife, had given Philip the key to her husband's beach house so that they could cook a late-night feast. Unfortunately, she forgot to tell the ambassador. As the lively party, cutlasses in teeth, scaled the cliffs to the house Sir Clifford Norton was heard to roar from an upstairs window, 'Who's there?' Later he changed out of his pyjamas and joined them as they cooked sausages.

By the spring of 1951 King George VI was seriously again ill. There was a shadow on his lung and the doctors suspected that he had cancer, although the royal family were not informed. Since the previous summer Princess Elizabeth had been allowed access to Cabinet papers and memoranda, to broaden her experience of state matters. She also read the daily Parliamentary reports to keep abreast of current affairs.

LOVE & MARRIAGE

In April, Elizabeth and Philip paid an official visit to Rome, where she found the sophisticated members of society rather intimidating. Wearing a long black dress and black veil, she paid a courtesy call at the Vatican. This sparked protests from Protestant groups in England, unhappy that the Pope had received the heiress presumptive in audience. In America the media focused on Italian criticism of the Princess's 'unfashionable' clothes. After the earlier triumph in Paris this unaccustomed censure was painful.

As Princess Elizabeth took on more of her father's duties, in July 1951 Philip was given indefinite leave from the Royal Navy and they returned from Malta for good.

A planned visit by George VI and Queen Elizabeth to Canada and the United States was postponed and instead, in September, the King underwent a bronchoscopy after a tumour was discovered on his left lung. The doctors' worst fears were confirmed when they found it to be malignant. On 23 September the lung was removed; a cautious bulletin was issued but by now it was obvious that the King would not survive much longer.

A General Election was pending and early in October an Order for the Prorogation of Parliament was approved at a meeting of the Privy Council, presided over by the Queen and Princess Elizabeth as Counsellors of State. The King, who uttered the word 'Approved' and signed the necessary documents from his sickbed, performed the final act of the Dissolution of Parliament. On 25 October, 76-year-old Winston Churchill led the Conservative Party to victory, ousting the post-war Labour Government of Clement Atlee.

It had been decided that the Duke and Duchess of Edinburgh would undertake the postponed official visit to Canada and the United States. On 7 October Elizabeth therefore became the first member of the royal family to fly across the Atlantic when she and Philip boarded a British Overseas Airways Corporation jet for the 17-hour flight to Montreal. As the King's life hung by a thread, amongst the pile of luggage were black mourning clothes and a sealed envelope containing the draft Accession Declaration. Elizabeth always had to be prepared for the worst.

In Canada they covered a distance of 10,000 miles, taking in every province in the dominion. A crowd of 25,000 people greeted them at Montreal airport, and half a million thronged the streets of Ottawa. But it was not all plain sailing: there were unfavourable comparisons with King George and Queen Elizabeth's triumphant visit in 1939. Canadians criticised the Princess because, unlike her ever-smiling mother, they felt she looked too glum.

Philip referred to Canada as 'a good investment', a remark that to some smacked of colonialism and caused offence. Yet there were moments of relaxation and sheer enjoyment. In Ottawa they threw themselves with gusto into a traditional square dance and were photographed spinning arm-in-arm, Elizabeth in a full skirt, Philip in a checked shirt and jeans. At Niagara Falls they donned protective clothing and went down to the viewing platform at the foot of the falls where, as *The Times* reported, 'they stood amid the thunder of the water with the spray drifting over them'.

Every day the Princess kept up with events by reading the airmail edition of *The Times*. She was naturally anxious about her father but on the long train journeys across Canada Philip attempted to lighten the mood by playing practical jokes, surprising her with a booby-trapped tin of nuts or chasing her down the corridor wearing a set of joke false teeth.

Washington, where they arrived by air on 31 October, was easier. As the White House was being redecorated they stayed at Blair House with President Truman, whose deaf, bedridden mother lived on the top floor. 'Mother, I've brought Princess Elizabeth to see you,' the President informed her. Having just heard that Churchill had been returned to power in the General Election the confused old lady told the Princess, 'I'm so glad your father's been re-elected.' On behalf of the King, Elizabeth presented gifts to mark the restoration of the White House.

CHAPTER 2

The Queen's Diamond Jubilee 43

LOVE & MARRIAGE

44 The Queen's Diamond Jubilee

CHAPTER 2

The 67-year-old President soon fell under Elizabeth's spell, describing her as a 'fairy princess' and in public relations terms alone the visit was deemed an unqualified success. 'As one father to another, we can be very proud of our daughters,' President Truman wrote to George VI.

On the Edinburghs' return to England in November the King made them both Privy Councillors. They were not reassured by his appearance. Martin Charteris, who had replaced Jock Colville as Elizabeth's private secretary in 1949, thought the King looked 'awful'. Nevertheless, on 2 December a 'Day of National Thanksgiving' for the King's recovery was celebrated before the entire royal family gathered at Sandringham as usual for Christmas.

On 29 January 1952 the King returned to London for a consultation with his doctors and the following evening the royal family ('Us Four and Philip' as the King called them) attended a performance of the musical *South Pacific* at Drury Lane Theatre.

The next day Elizabeth and Philip left London Airport for the tour of East Africa, Australia and New Zealand that the King had postponed in 1948. It would take them away for six months. The King stood on the tarmac, waving goodbye until his daughter's plane disappeared from view. Newsreel film showed him hatless in the cold wind, looking tired and drawn.

Their first stop was Nairobi, where they were driven through cheering crowds to Government House for a few days of official engagements, including a visit to Nairobi National Park where they photographed the wildlife. They were also officially presented with the key to Sagana Lodge, a cedar wood hunting lodge in the Aberdare Forest game reserve at Nyeri. The Kenyan people had given the lodge to them as a wedding present and on 3 February Elizabeth and Philip drove 100 miles over dusty roads to spend a few days resting there before the next stage of the tour.

On 5 February they decided to spend the night at nearby Treetops Hotel, set in the branches of a giant fig tree. It had only three bedrooms, a dining room and a room for the hunter but a specially constructed platform formed the perfect place from which to watch the wildlife. Although the hotel had been redecorated, baboons had lately forced their way inside and eaten some of the new lampshades. With Philip's equerry Michael Parker and Lady Pamela Mountbatten, who acted as Elizabeth's lady-in-waiting, they spent a fascinating night watching and filming elephants, baboons and rhinos at the watering hole and salt lick below. It was almost dawn before Elizabeth went to bed. Back at Sandringham, at some time during the early hours of 6 February, the King died peacefully in his sleep from thrombosis. Elizabeth had climbed up to Treetops as a princess but, unknowingly, she climbed down as queen. She is the only British sovereign in modern times whose exact moment of accession to the throne cannot be precisely timed.

The Queen's Diamond Jubilee 45

LOVE & MARRIAGE

Unaware of what had occurred, after breakfast Elizabeth and Philip drove back to Sagana Lodge to spend a few hours fishing before they left for Mombasa.

News of the King's death took a while to reach Kenya. His private secretary sent a telegram to Martin Charteris with the agreed code 'Hyde Park Corner' but it never arrived.

Meanwhile, an unconfirmed newsflash from Reuters arrived at the Outspan Hotel in Nyeri, the press headquarters for the royal visit, where Charteris was having lunch. Informed by a local journalist, he quickly telephoned Michael Parker, who found a radio and tuned in to the BBC. They were playing sombre music but there was no news. As Charteris drove back to Sagana Lodge, Parker made frantic telephone calls to obtain official confirmation.

LOVE & MARRIAGE

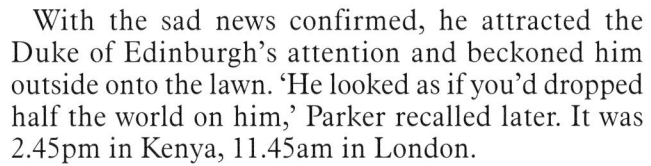

With the sad news confirmed, he attracted the Duke of Edinburgh's attention and beckoned him outside onto the lawn. 'He looked as if you'd dropped half the world on him,' Parker recalled later. It was 2.45pm in Kenya, 11.45am in London.

Philip found Elizabeth and took her outside towards the river, where they walked slowly up and down for a long time, trying to come to terms with what had happened. Inside, everyone was in a state of shock.

When Martin Charteris returned he found the new Queen sitting at her desk, calmly drafting telegrams of regret and apology for the cancellation of the remainder of the tour. Her cheeks were flushed but her eyes were dry. Years of royal training had prepared her well for this moment. Lady Pamela Mountbatten later recalled the contrast between the marvellous night they had just spent at Treetops and the morning's news, 'almost impossible to believe'.

Lady Pamela's instant reaction was sympathy for the young woman whose father had just died – 'it didn't sink in that it was the King,' she told author Elizabeth Longford. Typically, the new Queen's concern was for others. 'But I am so sorry that it means we've got to go back to England and it's upsetting everybody's plans,' she said.

While Michael Parker made arrangements for their immediate return to London, Martin Charteris opened the accession documents and asked by what name she wanted to be known as Queen. Twenty-five-year-old Elizabeth showed no hesitation. 'My own name, of course,' she replied. 'What else?

The Queen's Diamond Jubilee 49

50 The Queen's Diamond Jubilee

CHAPTER 3

The New Reign

by IAN LLOYD

ELIZABETH II'S FIRST act as Queen was to draft apologies to those awaiting her arrival in Australia and New Zealand. The royal party then had to make the 4,000-mile journey back to the United Kingdom, via Libya, arriving at London Airport on the afternoon of 7 February. There to greet the new monarch was her uncle, the Duke of Gloucester, her Prime Minister Winston Churchill and the Leader of the Opposition, Clement Attlee.

The Queen arrived at Clarence House at 4pm. Half an hour later, her 84-year-old grandmother Queen Mary drove across from nearby Marlborough House. 'Her old Grannie,' she said, 'must be the first to kiss her hand.'

The Queen's official life began the following morning with her accession council at St James's Palace. She told the assembled politicians that she aimed to continue her father's work. 'I pray that God will help me to discharge worthily the heavy task that has been laid upon me so early in my life.'

THE NEW REIGN

Only then, after carrying out the duties of a monarch, could Elizabeth mourn as a daughter and travel to Sandringham to be reunited with her widowed mother and her children, three-year-old Charles and Anne, 18 months.

For the Queen and the Duke of Edinburgh the move to Buckingham Palace was a tremendous wrench as by then they had settled comfortably into the newly refurbished Clarence House. Philip proposed that the Queen Mother stay at the palace while they continued to live at Clarence House and use the palace only as an office. But Sir Alan Lascelles, George VI's Private Secretary who now served the new Queen in the same capacity, had other ideas.

Buckingham Palace was the seat of monarchy and the Queen must move in. He also had the backing of Churchill, who said simply: 'To the Palace they must go.' It was a kick in the teeth for Prince Philip, who soon realised his position as consort clearly counted for little against the combined strength of the old guard.

52 The Queen's Diamond Jubilee

CHAPTER 3

The Queen's Diamond Jubilee 53

THE NEW REIGN

54 The Queen's Diamond Jubilee

An even greater blow to the Duke's confidence came just days after the accession. Earl Mountbatten had been crowing at a house party 'the House of Mountbatten now reigned'. Prince Ernst August of Hanover, a grandson of Kaiser Wilhelm II, was a fellow guest and later reported the conversation to Queen Mary. Her husband had of course founded the House of Windsor in 1917, and on hearing that the very name of the royal dynasty was being challenged, she sent for Jock Colville, Churchill's Private Secretary.

Churchill backed Queen Mary and in April Queen Elizabeth II signed an order in council that stated: 'I and my children shall be styled and known as the House of Windsor.' 'I am nothing but a bloody amoeba,' Philip memorably protested. 'I am the only man in the country not allowed to give his name to his own children.'

Queen Mary did not have long to live. She died on 24 March 1953, having outlived three of her sons, and had to cope with what, to her, was arguably an even greater blow, the abdication of a fourth.

The rest of that spring was taken up with final preparations for the Queen's Coronation on 2 June. Prince Philip had been made chairman of the Coronation Commission, which in part made up for the slights he had received the previous year.

Jock Colville wrote in his diary: 'Never has there been such excitement, never has the monarch received such adulation.' As a result of a change of heart by the Queen quite late in the proceedings the ceremony was televised live, giving millions of her subjects a ringside seat for this most ancient of ceremonies. Sales of television sets soared as a result.

A massive crowd, estimated at 12 deep in parts, had slept for several nights in The Mall and all along the processional route. Although the date had been chosen because statistically it had the most recorded sunshine on record, it rain heavily during much of the proceedings. But the inclement weather failed to dampen the enthusiasm of onlookers, especially when that morning's newspapers brought the welcome news that a British expedition led by Captain John Hunt had conquered Mount Everest. Edmund Hillary, a New Zealand beekeeper, had been the first to set foot on the summit with Sherpa Tenzing Norgay. One headline summed up the euphoria: 'All This And Everest Too!'

The coronation of a queen regnant differs from that of a king in one crucial aspect: her consort is not crowned alongside her. The Duke of Edinburgh was a bystander like the rest of the royal family. His only part in the ceremony was when he knelt before her and promised to become her 'liege man of life and limb, and of earthly worship... So help me God'.

They travelled in the Gold State Coach to and from Westminster Abbey. A further 27 carriages, 29 military bands and some 13,000 troops took part in the various processions, providing an unforgettable spectacle for the rain-soaked masses. 'Not a bad show,' as the Duke of Edinburgh succinctly put it.

One small detail could have ruined Coronation Day. As members of the royal family gathered in a specially built annexe at the front of the abbey, the *Daily Mirror*'s royal reporter, Audrey Whiting, noticed Princess Margaret gently brush a fleck of dust off the uniform of Group Captain Peter Townsend before running her fingers across his medals. Townsend, an equerry to the late King, was now comptroller of the Queen Mother's household.

The implication of the Princess's intimate gesture was clear to Whiting: Margaret was in love and not afraid to show it. The reporter tore back to her office to inform her editor that she had the real story of the day; however, in those more deferential times he refused to run it, telling Whiting he wouldn't spoil the Queen's special day.

THE NEW REIGN

The love affair between the Queen's sister and the divorced Battle of Britain hero had begun in the immediate aftermath of King George's death, which left 21-year-old Margaret bereft and without the sense of direction that her sister obviously now had. With Lilibet occupied in her new role and the Queen Mother distracted by widowhood and the impending move to Clarence House, Margaret sought solace in the handsome Townsend.

Shortly before the Coronation, Margaret told her mother and sister that she was in love and wanted to marry. The Queen Mother, once dubbed 'the imperial ostrich' for her ability to put distasteful matters out of her mind, did nothing. The Queen asked her sister to put matters on hold. 'Under the circumstances,' she said, 'it isn't unreasonable for me to ask you to wait a year.' The news broke in mid-June when the *People* newspaper ran a front-page story revealing the speculation printed by its foreign counterparts.

Meanwhile, hoping that distance might lessen the couple's infatuation, the Palace arranged for Townsend to have a posting in Brussels for two years as an air attaché. Margaret, on a tour of Rhodesia with her mother at the time, was furious that she wasn't even allowed to say goodbye.

Two years later, when the Princess reached the age of 25, under the terms of the 1772 Royal Marriages Act she would be free to marry Townsend without the consent of the Queen, providing she could secure the approval of Parliament. In doing so, she would lose her Civil List annuity and her position as third in line to the throne.

THE NEW REIGN

The dilemma was similar to the one faced by her uncle, King Edward VIII, a generation earlier. This time, however, duty came before personal fulfilment. On 31 October 1955, Margaret announced that 'mindful of the church's teaching that Christian marriage is indissoluble, and conscious of my duty to the Commonwealth, I have resolved to put these considerations before others'. The Princess gave up the man she loved rather than face a life of exile and ostracism.

Some biographers have suggested that concerns about Margaret's private life led to the Palace and Churchill colluding to create the 1953 Regency Act. This was approved by Parliament in November and stated that in the event of the Queen's death, Prince Philip would act as regent until Prince Charles came of age. Under the terms of the previous 1937 Act, the regent would have been the next adult member of the royal family in line to the throne, i.e. Princess Margaret.

The same month the Regency Act was approved, the Queen and Duke set off on a five-and-a-half month tour of the Commonwealth, to enable as many as possible of Her Majesty's overseas subjects to see her during this first post-Coronation overseas visit.

The mammoth imperial progress included tours of Bermuda, Jamaica, Fiji. Tonga, the Coco Islands, Aden, Uganda, Malta and Gibraltar. The couple spent three months in Australia and New Zealand and 10 days in Ceylon, and the Queen wore her Coronation dress to open Parliament in each of these countries. She would wear it once more in 1957 when she also opened Parliament in Canada.

The Queen and her husband travelled 44,000 miles by air, sea and land on the 1953-4 tour, and it was estimated that three quarters of the population of Australia turned out to catch a glimpse – albeit a distant one – of their monarch. For the only time in her life, Elizabeth spent Christmas outside the UK and made her annual broadcast live from Auckland, New Zealand. On her arrival in that country the Maoris hailed her as 'The Rare White Heron of the Single Flight'.

On their return journey the couple were joined by Prince Charles and Princess Anne in Malta. The children had sailed to meet their mother on the new Royal Yacht *Britannia*, which Elizabeth had launched on Clydeside in April 1953. It would serve the Queen and Duke as a floating palace for over four decades.

Previous monarchs had left part of their legacy in the homes they built: Queen Victoria and Prince Albert designed Balmoral Castle and Osborne House, while their eldest son, the future Edward VII, was responsible for Sandringham House in Norfolk. *Britannia* was the nearest Elizabeth and Philip came to creating a 'home' from scratch, and her obvious attachment to it was plainly visible as she fought back tears on the day the yacht was decommissioned in 1997.

CHAPTER 3

The Queen's Diamond Jubilee 59

THE NEW REIGN

Hugh Casson, who had recently designed Philip's study and library at the palace, was commissioned to design *Britannia*'s interior. In his diary he noted the Queen asked him to keep costs down while maintaining a sense of tradition in the design, and much of the furniture from the previous yacht, *Victoria and Albert*, was used.

'The idea was to give the impression of a country house at sea,' Casson recalled. 'The Queen is a meticulous observer with very strong views on everything from the door-handles to the shape of the lampshades'.

In 1956 Prince Philip founded the Duke of Edinburgh Award Scheme, arguably his greatest achievement. Since then, some two-and-a-half million young people have taken part and have benefited from the scheme that puts an emphasis on self-reliance, enterprise and endeavour.

The early years weren't easy for the Duke, whose radical, modernising attitude often met resistance from the deeply entrenched conservatism of courtiers. His cousin Patricia, now Countess Mountbatten of Burma, recalled Philip in the 1950s as 'a dynamo, an absolute dynamo', while her husband Lord Brabourne pointed out Philip found the attitude of the palace old guard 'intolerable and deeply frustrating'.

In October 1956, Philip set off on a solo four-month tour that took him to Australia, New Zealand, Ceylon, the Gambia, Antarctica and the Falkland Islands. Biographers have suggested this was a sign the Duke had reached the limit of endurance with life at court, while others suggest his marriage may have been in trouble. More than 40 years later it was still a sensitive subject. When Channel 4 television produced a two-part documentary entitled *The Real Prince Philip* in 1999, his then private secretary, Brigadier Miles Hunt-Davis, wrote to the film's producers to voice his displeasure at the coverage of the 1956 tour. 'Your portrayal was marred... firstly by implying that the journey was undertaken to get away from the Queen and the court and secondly that it was a spree. This is totally wrong,' he wrote. 'The journey was planned to allow His Royal Highness to open the Olympic Games in Melbourne and the use of *Britannia* was to enable Prince Philip to visit as many of the remote British Dependent Islands as possible.'

Nonetheless, in retrospect it is hard not to conclude that something was amiss. When the royal couple were reunited in Portugal in February 1957 Philip emerged from his aeroplane wearing a tie with love hearts on it, which made headlines in the following day's newspapers. The same month the Queen announced that her husband had been granted the title 'Prince of the United Kingdom', something that had been overlooked when he was created Duke of Edinburgh on the eve of his wedding. Churchill originally suggested this to the Cabinet in 1955, though it was another prime minister, Harold Macmillan, who claimed the credit for introducing it in 1957; what he didn't say was that it knocked the rumours of a rift in the royal marriage by making the Queen be seen to publicly reward her husband.

While the Duke was overseas, the Queen was involved with the greatest political crisis of her reign thus far. In January 1957 her second Prime Minister, Anthony Eden, saw the Queen at Sandringham to tell her his doctors had advised him to step down as Premier. Elizabeth now had to choose a leader from the Conservative party that was still split over Britain's aborted intervention in the Suez crisis the previous year.

Two candidates emerged: 'Rab' Butler, who had deputised for the ailing Eden, and Harold Macmillan, the Chancellor of the Exchequer. Although Butler was regarded by many as the favourite, the Conservatives in those days had no mechanism for electing a leader. Instead, two peers took informal soundings within the government whilst Edward Heath, the chief whip, did the same with other Tory MPs.

One of the peers, Lord Salisbury, went to see the Queen on 10 January to tell her that most government ministers and MPs backed Macmillan. The Queen also sought advice from Sir Winston Churchill, who had retired two years earlier, and he backed the findings, so Elizabeth sent for Macmillan at 2pm that same day and asked him to form a government.

Later that year there was a personal attack on the Queen and her advisers, which by today's standards seems inconsequential but in those deferential times made headlines. In the edition of the *National and English Review* published on 31 August 1957, its editor, Lord Altrincham, lashed out at the way the Palace was running things.

The Queen, he wrote, came over as 'a priggish schoolgirl, captain of the hockey team', who he went on to say, 'is unable to string a few sentences together without a written text'. Altrincham dismissed courtiers as 'tweedy' and 'a tight little enclave of English ladies and gentlemen'.

Fleet Street naturally delighted in reporting the furore this generated. Altrincham was slapped across the face by an outraged middle-aged man as he left a television studio, while the Queen's cousin, the Earl of Strathmore, announced: 'Altrincham should be shot!'

Two months later, journalist Malcolm Muggeridge described the royal family as 'a soap opera, a sort of substitute or ersatz religion' in an article in the *Saturday Evening Post*. As a result of his comments, Muggeridge was fired from the BBC, sacked as a columnist and had to resign from his club.

THE NEW REIGN

62 The Queen's Diamond Jubilee

Around the same time, one of the original 'Angry Young Men', the playwright John Osborne, wrote in *The Times*: 'My objection to the Royal Family is that it is dead: it is a gold filling in a mouth full of decay.'

Such comments made a mere five years into the new reign were sensational at the time. They forced courtiers to re-evaluate their role and whether by coincidence or not several changes were made. The archaic tradition of presentations at court, where the ruling classes could parade their daughters in front of the monarch, was abolished the following year. Decades later, Princess Margaret gave her own interpretation: 'We had to stop it,' she said, 'because every tart in London was getting in.'

The Queen was also hosting informal luncheon parties at which she got to meet people from all walks of life, though to be fair this initiative came about before Altrincham *et al* had vented their criticisms.

Later in 1957 another initiative brought the monarch into closer contact with her subjects when the Queen's Christmas broadcast was televised for the first time. It proved a popular move and the following autumn the State Opening of Parliament was also televised.

A shy and nervous eight-year-old Prince Charles arrived at Cheam Preparatory School in September of that year, having journeyed from Scotland with his parents on the Royal Train. The move made history, with Charles becoming the first royal heir to be educated outside palace walls.

The previous January he had enrolled as a day pupil at Hill House in Knightsbridge, but now he would be a boarder, separated from his family for a whole term. The Palace ignored Labour MPs' calls to have Charles educated at a state school. The choice was very much Prince Philip's, who had himself been a pupil at Cheam in the 1930s.

The following July, Charles was called to the headmaster's study to watch the closing ceremony of the 1958 Commonwealth Games at Cardiff Arms Park. The Queen had been due to attend but was confined to bed with sinusitis. Instead, a recorded message was relayed to the 36,000-strong crowd.

The Queen's Diamond Jubilee 63

THE NEW REIGN

The Queen said the games 'made this a memorable year for the principality'. Then to everyone's surprise, she announced: 'I have decided to mark it further by an act which will, I hope, give as much pleasure to all Welshmen as it does to me. I intend to make my son Charles, Prince of Wales today.'

The rest of her words were drowned out by cheers as she promised: 'When he is grown up, I will present him to you at Caernarfon.'

During the 1950s the Queen and the Duke of Edinburgh undertook several major overseas tours. It is difficult for younger generations to comprehend the effect they had at the time. Not only had previous 20th-century monarchs been more remote figures but they also lacked Elizabeth and Philip's glamorous appeal, which was ideally suited to the burgeoning television age.

In 1956 the royal couple toured Nigeria, arriving on 28 January to a tremendous welcome. The following day, when they attended Sunday worship in Lagos, the surging crowds bent metal posts in their enthusiasm. The tour was memorable for the Queen's visit to a leper colony, the 1950s equivalent of the Princess of Wales's involvement with AIDS charities 30 years later.

Local drums beat out the message 'Our mother is coming!' as the royal party arrived at the colony. The Queen and her husband agreed to adopt a leper child financially, much to the delight of the organisation's supervisor. 'The visit will do more to conquer man's fear and hate of the disease than any other single act I can think of,' he said.

64 The Queen's Diamond Jubilee

CHAPTER 3

The Queen's Diamond Jubilee 65

THE NEW REIGN

As well as carrying out overseas tours on behalf of the United Kingdom, the Queen and the Duke, then as now, hosted one or two incoming state visits each year. The first of her reign was in June 1954 when King Gustaf VI and Queen Louise of Sweden arrived for a four-day stay. This was also a family occasion since Louise was Prince Philip's maternal aunt.

Later the same year, Emperor Haile Selassie of Ethiopia visited. He was welcomed to the country by the Duke of Gloucester, who had attended Selassie's coronation service in Addis Ababa in 1930. That evening the Queen hosted a state banquet in his honour at Buckingham Palace.

The mention of Selassie's visit is a reminder to the 21st-century reader that at the beginning of the Queen's 60-year reign she was the contemporary of political leaders who were, more often than not, older than her parents. The Ethiopian Emperor had, after all, first dined at Buckingham Palace in 1924 as a guest of King George V.

Elizabeth's first Prime Minister, Winston Churchill, was born in 1874 and had fought for her great-great-grandmother, Queen Victoria, at the Battle of Omdurman in 1898. At the time of her accession in 1952, Harry S. Truman was President of the United States, Chiang Kai-Shek was the ruler of China, and Joseph Stalin was head of state in the USSR.

66 The Queen's Diamond Jubilee

CHAPTER 3

The Queen's Diamond Jubilee 67

THE NEW REIGN

The Queen's first outward state visit was another family occasion and a link to a bygone age. In June 1955, she and Prince Philip arrived in Oslo aboard *Britannia* for a three-day visit hosted by King Haakon VII of Norway. Born Prince Carl of Denmark in 1872, Haakon was a son-in-law of the Queen's great-grandfather, Edward VII, and a nephew of Queen Alexandra. In 1896 he had married his cousin Princess Maud of Wales in the chapel at Buckingham Palace. Nine years later he was invited to become King of Norway.

The Queen has met all US presidents since Harry Truman, apart from Lyndon Johnson. In October 1957 she paid her first visit to the USA as monarch and attended a banquet at the White House hosted by Dwight D. Eisenhower. During that visit she addressed the United Nations General Assembly, an honour she would repeat exactly half a century later in 2007.

Media interest in the young Queen was intense, and some 3,000 journalists and photographers were accredited to cover the tour. Elizabeth's press secretary, Commander Richard Colville, dubbed 'The Abominable "No" Man' by Fleet Street for his uncooperative attitude, managed to keep most of them as far away as possible.

'As far as we can tell, she is human,' *The Washington Post* commented sarcastically, but *The Chicago Daily News* was more upbeat, declaring the monarch 'a doll, a living doll'.

CHAPTER 3

THE NEW REIGN

The last major tour of the decade was to Canada in June and July of 1959. During her gruelling 45-day visit she opened the St Lawrence Seaway in the presence of Eisenhower and the Canadian Prime Minister, John Diefenbaker.

Most unusually, the Queen had to pull out of some of her engagements. Unknown to all but a few members of the royal party, 33-year-old Elizabeth was in the early stages of her third pregnancy and understandably found the constant humidity a trial. News of the Queen's condition was released on her return to Britain.

During the autumn months she withdrew from public life, as was the custom for royal ladies in those days. As the 1950s ended, Her Majesty and her family were at Sandringham House, where they saw in the New Year and looked forward to a new decade and – more importantly – a new addition to the family.

72 The Queen's Diamond Jubilee

CHAPTER 4

The 1960s

by LUCINDA GOSLING

THE 'SWINGING SIXTIES' began quietly for the Queen. She was pregnant with her third child and, seven weeks into the fledgling decade, Prince Andrew Albert Christian Edward made his appearance, born at Buckingham Palace on 19 February 1960 weighing 7lb 3oz. This new royal baby, who arrived almost 10 years after his sister Anne, brought joy and delight to the 33-year-old Queen, who described her baby son as 'adorable' in a letter to her cousin, Lady Mary Cambridge, adding, 'the children are riveted by him' and thought he would be 'very spoilt'.

This 'second family' seemed to herald a more modern and relaxed era of parenting for the Queen and Prince Philip. 'Goodness,' said Her Majesty to a friend, 'what fun it is to have a baby in the house again'; eight years into her reign, she seemed more confident of herself and her ability to switch between the incongruous roles of monarch and mother. She admitted her favourite night of the week was 'Mabel's night off' when the royal nanny, Mabel Anderson, took a break.

Prince Andrew's arrival coincided with another happy family event when, later that month, an engagement was announced. Princess Margaret was to marry society photographer Antony Armstrong-Jones. The Queen's younger sister had endured an ill-fated and very public romance with Group Captain Peter Townsend in the previous decade – a potential *mésalliance* whose conclusion was, due to Townsend's divorced status, almost inevitably one of sacrifice and disappointment. While ministers and courtiers had meddled in Margaret's love life in 1955, the Queen avoided clashing with her sister over the issue, offering neither criticism nor encouragement – a stance that many say is characteristic of her when difficult decisions need to be made. In the end, Margaret chose duty over happiness and in the process earned widespread public sympathy for her plight.

THE 1960s

The Queen no doubt breathed a sigh of relief that the 'Margaret problem' was to find a satisfactory solution, although the comparatively humble origins of the Princess's fiancé raised eyebrows. Harold Macmillan, with a comedic flourish, described an encounter with the Queen's uncle, the Duke of Gloucester, after arriving at Sandringham early in 1960. 'Thank heavens you've come, Prime Minister,' said Harry Gloucester. 'The Queen's in a terrible state; there's a fellow called Jones in the billiard room wants to marry her sister, and Prince Philip's in the library wanting to change the family name to Mountbatten!'

Although to modern eyes Armstrong-Jones's pedigree was distinctly upper-class – he had gone to Eton and his mother's second marriage had made her Countess of Rosse – the thought of a royal so close to the throne choosing an untitled photographer as her spouse would have caused consternation a generation earlier. But after the Townsend debacle, there were no objections to this likeable young man who might at last offer some happiness to the Princess. Besides, a member of the family who worked for his living in an occupation that was to gain huge kudos in the 1960s was hugely positive for the image of the monarchy.

The royal wedding, the first to be televised, was held at Westminster Abbey on 6 May. Princess Margaret looked ravishing in a simple but sumptuous Hartnell gown, the Poltimore tiara twinkling under the powerful television lights. Enhanced by the poised and lyrical commentary of Richard Dimbleby, the atmosphere of feverish excitement and sentimental romance underscoring the day was to set the tone for future royal nuptials.

Time would show that Margaret's fairy-tale wedding did not have the requisite happy ending and it demonstrated that royal marriages were as fallible as any other. But for now the Princess appeared very much in love. In fact, the early 1960s saw a cluster of royal weddings – the Queen's cousin, the Duke of Kent, married Katharine Worsley at York Minster in 1961, while his sister Princess Alexandra married the Honourable Angus Ogilvy at Westminster Abbey two years later.

CHAPTER 4

The Queen's Diamond Jubilee 75

THE 1960s

CHAPTER 4

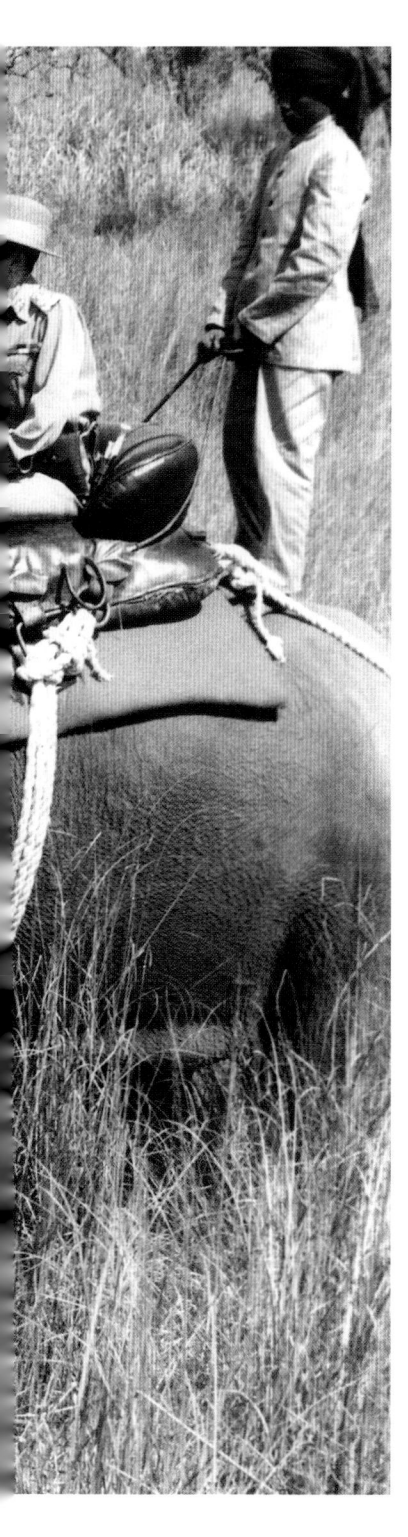

Prince Andrew's imminent arrival revived the festering issue of royal surnames. Back in 1952, the Duke of Edinburgh had been keen to incorporate his surname with the Windsor family name; the proposal was blocked by the then Prime Minister, Winston Churchill, who, more than anything was adamant that the Mountbattens, headed by Prince Philip's scheming uncle Dickie, should not give their name to the ruling house of Great Britain.

In December 1959, the Queen, keen to give her husband equal status on at least one count, raised the issue with Harold Macmillan, who was aware of the outspoken opinions from various quarters, most publicly the Bishop of Carlisle, who argued that a royal baby should have as much right as any other to bear its father's name.

Just eight days before Andrew's birth, an announcement was made stating that any descendant of the Queen through the male line not of Royal Highness status would use the surname Mountbatten-Windsor. The Earl of Wessex's daughter, Lady Louise, is the first member of the royal family to do so. The resolution, said the Queen, gave her 'great peace of mind' and no doubt gave Dickie, whose wife Edwina died suddenly just two days after Prince Andrew's birth, some sense of satisfaction.

The Queen and Prince Philip's youngest child, Prince Edward, was born in March 1964, completing a family that was the very picture of domestic harmony. Her Majesty was very close to Princess Margaret's children, David and Sarah, born in 1961 and 1964 respectively, who were frequently seen in the company of their Windsor cousins. The Queen Mother was still spry in her sixties (she would, after all, live for another three decades), and with teenage as well as younger children the Queen's family could claim to represent every age group in society.

Elizabeth II was the first reigning monarch to have a baby since Queen Victoria gave birth to her youngest child, Princess Beatrice, in 1857. Inevitably, her third pregnancy resulted in some diary reshuffling and rescheduling, not least a long-planned official tour to Ghana in West Africa, one of several countries that had become independent in recent years but remained in the Commonwealth. She dispatched her private secretary Martin Charteris to Accra to explain the situation to Prime Minister Kwame Nkrumah in confidence. The tour was postponed until 1961, by which time Ghana's self-rule was sliding into a dictatorship and there were rumblings of anti-British feeling triggering genuine anxiety about the safety of such a trip for the Queen.

The Queen's Diamond Jubilee 77

THE 1960s

78 The Queen's Diamond Jubilee

Here was a dilemma for the British government. Should the Head of the Commonwealth stay protected at home and not be seen to tolerate a regime that severely curtailed civil liberties, or should she carry out her duties: working for the Commonwealth and showing the kind of moral fibre for which her parents were renowned during the Second World War? The Queen on her part wished to go, but remained passive while government officials prevaricated about the right approach.

Her Private Secretary, Michael Adeane, wrote of the Queen's reaction: 'She is personally unmoved by this sort of thing.' The visit, which gave Macmillan sleepless nights, passed without incident and was declared a success, perhaps something the Queen secretly knew it would be all along.

Ghana was not the only controversial visit the Queen undertook during the 1960s. Her trip to Canada in 1964, her return to public duty after the birth of Prince Edward, was tainted in the light of an upsurge of Quebec separatism, with the possibility of highly disruptive demonstrations and even death threats directed at the monarch. In this case, the Canadian government took a hard-line approach to the demonstrators, charging the crowd and arresting large numbers of protestors. Unsurprisingly, the Queen was booed during one procession.

Conversely, the reaction from the host nation during a state visit to Germany in May 1965 was remarkably positive. It was the first visit by a British monarch since George V attended the marriage of his cousin Princess Viktoria Luise of Prussia in 1913. Coming 20 years after the end of the Second World War, the wounds of conflict had not quite healed and the visit was approached cautiously by the Queen who, concerned about public opinion, made it clear she would only embark on such a visit on the advice of the government. After several invitations from Germany, the British government felt they could not avoid the subject any longer and so the Queen and Prince Philip set off. The reaction from the German population was one of delight and jubilation; they viewed the British monarch's extended hand of friendship as a symbolic first stage in their country's rehabilitation and acceptance by countries that had been enemies for much of the 20th century.

THE 1960s

A continual thorn in the government's side during the 1960s was Southern Rhodesia, now Zimbabwe. In November 1965, the administration of Ian Smith, whose Rhodesian Front party opposed black majority rule in the British colony, signed a unilateral declaration of independence of Rhodesia from the United Kingdom but maintained an allegiance to Elizabeth II. Under Mr Smith's system there would be white minority rule, where 220,000 white Rhodesians enjoyed electoral privileges over nearly four million black Rhodesians. In response, the British government implemented a range of sanctions: these included ceasing all British aid to Rhodesia and preferential treatment for the country, banning the import of Rhodesian tobacco and recalling the British High Commissioner.

Smith continued to regard the Queen as a separate entity to her government, but this stubborn view placed them in an awkward position. Distancing herself from the Smith regime required personal communication but to be seen to contact Smith separately from her government by its very nature made her appear independent of it. She refused to accept the title Queen of Rhodesia, and eventually the Smith government abandoned attempts to remain loyal to the Crown. In 1969, a majority of the electorate voted in a referendum to declare Rhodesia a republic.

Incoming state visits were not always free from debate. In London in July 1963, King Paul I and Queen Frederica of Greece were met with protests against the Greek government's civil rights record and Frederica's right-wing involvements. Prince Philip's familial connections to the Greek royal family (Paul was his cousin) added extra embarrassment to the visit. The royal party were jeered outside the Aldwych Theatre, where they attended a play. The Home Secretary, Henry Brooke, was incensed. 'I never thought such a thing would happen in Britain,' he wrote. 'I don't know when it last happened in this country that a reigning monarch was given such treatment.'

In fact, such treatment of the royals was symptomatic of a growing combination of political activism and a 'satire boom' that was beginning to gnaw away at the long-held deferential monarchist tradition. It was not directed at the royal family specifically but it was part of a trend where the increasingly permissive 1960s' society began to question – and often mock – what it perceived to be outmoded and stuffy institutions, of which the monarchy was one. A famous scene in the BBC's late-night satirical programme *That Was The Week That Was* showed the Windsor family aboard a sinking royal barge with a pompous commentator delivering a deadpan description of the Queen's outfit.

CHAPTER 4

The Queen's Diamond Jubilee 81

THE 1960s

Private Eye magazine, launched in 1961, pictured the Queen opening Parliament on its cover with a thought bubble making it clear, in scatological terms, that she had made no personal contribution to her speech. It was hardly *Spitting Image*, a satirical puppet show that aired in Britain in the 1980s and 1990s, but it reflected a perceptible shift in the public mood. In the same year that the Profumo Scandal brought the Conservative government to its knees, it seemed that being royal – or in a position of power – was no longer a guarantee of respect.

Notable among this generation was a young Member of Parliament called Anthony Wedgwood Benn. The son of a Liberal Minister of Parliament, Benn's reputation preceded him after he had campaigned against hereditary titles, and suggested that ministers visiting Buckingham Palace should dispense with dinner jackets and travel around in the new Mini car. In 1964, the Conservatives under Alec Douglas-Home (a friend of the royal family) were defeated and the Queen welcomed Harold Wilson, a grammar school-educated pipe-smoker – along with several members of his family – through the doors of Buckingham Palace and invited him to form a government.

Under Wilson, Benn was given the position of Postmaster General, a role in which one might think it was difficult to implement any radical republican policies, but the new minister had other ideas. His singular aim was to remove the Queen's head from British stamps. He recorded in his diary the day he took a set of headless designs to the Palace to show the Queen, who politely showed interest during a 40-minute audience while Benn spread them out on the carpet for her perusal.

The Postmaster General left the palace on a high. 'I went back to the House of Commons feeling absolutely on top of the world,' he noted in his diary, but the Queen had simply conducted herself as she generally had taught herself to do so in public – she had disguised her true feelings and left the negotiations to be handled by her private secretaries.

THE 1960s

His optimism had turned to despondency by late 1965, writing in his diary this time, 'the plain fact is, that I shan't get the Queen's head off the stamps. And it is probably rather foolish of me to keep on knocking my head against a brick wall.' The one concession to Benn's proposed changes was that the Queen's head was reduced in size for commemorative stamps.

The tussle over the stamp issue revealed a woman adept at avoiding confrontation but nevertheless expert at resolutely ensuring that when matters meant a lot to her she had a steely determination. But the mere existence of personalities like Tony Benn, who were not afraid to challenge and question the institution of the monarchy, suggested that some recognition of this and some modernisation might benefit the royals.

The 1960s were a time of social, cultural and political change. Cecil Beaton's iconic photograph of the Queen in her coronation robes might have been the defining image of the 1950s, but The Beatles, Harold Wilson and miniskirts were the icons of the following 10 years. Hardy Amies, perhaps the Queen's favourite designer, bemoaned the rising hemlines of the period, complaining that it was impossible to dress the monarch with any dignity with such a diminished skirt length. Then as now, the Queen had to rise above fashion.

CHAPTER 4

The Queen's Diamond Jubilee 85

THE 1960s

Modernisation came in another form, with the arrival of a young Australian called William Heseltine at the palace press office in 1964. He would eventually replace the loyal but largely intransigent Commander Colville.

Having also served as Press Secretary to King George VI, Colville had a reputation in Fleet Street of being a 'No' man, seeing his role as quite simply to protect the royal family and to restrict the press as much as possible. Heseltine, on the other hand, realised that the royal family needed the press just as much as the press needed the royal family, a public-relations philosophy which in Buckingham Palace was close to revolutionary.

Under Heseltine's influence, the Queen's Christmas broadcast was transmitted in colour for the first time and, in 1967, when British yachtsman Francis Chichester returned from sailing around the world single-handedly, his knighting was carried out most publicly in Greenwich using the sword Elizabeth I had used to knight Francis Drake in 1580. This was a bonding of historic royal pageantry with a new publicity-friendly approach from the Palace and was created almost exclusively with cameras in mind.

The royal family's experimentation with publicity found its full expression at the end of the decade when they starred in their own documentary, *Royal Family*. The film, which aimed to show the Queen and her family 'off-duty', arose from discussions between Heseltine and Lord Mountbatten's film director son-in-law, Lord Brabourne.

Prince Philip, always a modernising influence within 'The Firm' in comparison with his more cautious wife, got behind the project. The Queen agreed to the proposal with the stricture that she could veto the results if they were not to her liking.

CHAPTER 4

The Queen's Diamond Jubilee 87

From Heseltine's point of view, this was a chance to set the record straight in an age when reports on the royal family were becoming increasingly misleading, and to harness the power of television for the royal family's own ends. 'There was nothing between the Court Circular and the gossip columns,' he later recalled. Furthermore, simply by embracing the medium of television and allowing a fly-on-the-wall documentary to record their daily lives, the Queen went some way towards shedding the dull, out-of-touch reputation the monarchy had acquired.

Whether the film achieved all this is debatable, but there was no doubt that it stirred up a voyeuristic interest among the Queen's subjects; when it was transmitted in June 1969, viewing figures estimated that 68 per cent of the British population watched the programme. Richard Cawston, Head of Documentaries at the BBC, was chosen to direct the film, spending a year with the royal family and shooting 43 hours of footage that were eventually pared down to a one-and-a-half-hour film. It showed Her Majesty skipping between public and private life, from a state visit to South America to Christmas at Windsor and a somewhat contrived scene by a loch at Balmoral where the Queen, Prince Philip and their children prepared a barbecue.

The film was a double-edged sword. On the one hand, the public were fascinated by this unprecedented invitation to observe the royal family at close quarters, to hear them speak informally to each other and to even share a joke. The Queen was seen discussing the banalities of what to wear with her dresser, Bobo Macdonald, and buying an ice cream for Prince Edward in the shop near Balmoral. It showed fully-formed individuals with personalities of their own and was proof that the Queen did in fact work rather hard (dealing with her red boxes and state papers was and still is a key feature of her daily life). Here was a woman whose life demanded far more of her than merely waving from cars or carriages.

But the film, while initiated by the Palace, also went a long way towards diminishing the mystique of royalty, which Heseltine's predecessor had devoted his life to protecting and upholding. *Royal Family* allowed the world to spend time with the Queen on the Palace's terms, and despite relative editorial freedom the programme had been carefully constructed to paint a positive portrait of the monarchy.

But it made the royal family the subject of public scrutiny. The Crown was no longer the revered and remote institution it once was, and the gentlemanly agreement of Fleet Street to treat it as such vanished. As the following decades would show, ignoring the media was impossible and press intrusion into royal life would, at times, have disastrous consequences.

CHAPTER 4

The Queen's Diamond Jubilee 89

THE 1960s

Certainly, the 1960s saw the Queen faced with many challenges where public expectation clashed with private feelings. On 21 October 1966, the South Wales mining village of Aberfan suffered an unimaginable tragedy when a coal tip collapsed, engulfing a primary school and killing 116 children and 28 adults. It remains one of the bleakest moments in recent British history.

The Queen's brother-in-law, Lord Snowdon, went immediately to the area to offer support to bereaved families. Her husband followed a day later, but the Queen, despite the country's expectation, did not visit Aberfan until eight days after the disaster. Never given to impetuous gestures, and repulsed by the idea of having to 'play-act' demonstrable emotion for the cameras, she pointed out that her presence would hamper the rescue effort.

'People will be looking after me. So perhaps they'll miss some poor child that might have been found under the wreckage.' There was no doubt that the tragedy affected her deeply, as a mother herself, but she was criticised – in the same way she was following the death of the Princess of Wales in 1997 – for not acting sooner.

The Queen's naturally reserved and reflective character is often mistaken for emotional repression but she has in fact returned twice to Aberfan since the tragedy, making it clear that her caring nature is manifested in careful, considered actions rather than spontaneous gestures.

Another area of scrutiny has been that of her relationship with her eldest son, Prince Charles, who, from his perspective at least, had an unhappy education during the 1960s, first at Cheam, his prep school in Surrey, and

90 The Queen's Diamond Jubilee

CHAPTER 4

then at Prince Philip's *alma mater*, Gordonstoun, in Morayshire, Scotland. It was a matter on which the Queen deferred to her husband, who had flourished in the sporty and Spartan environment of the school; their decision to send their son away to be educated was probably no different to that made by the majority of upper-class parents at the time.

For the sensitive and shy Charles, however, the regime was very tough. Nevertheless, he acclimatised, taking part in school plays, his father's Duke of Edinburgh Award scheme, and becoming proficient at the cello. He left with a clutch of O-levels.

An anecdote from the Labour MP Barbara Castle, who attended a banquet at Buckingham Palace during a state visit by the President of Chile in 1967, shows that the Queen experienced the same anxieties as any mother at the thought of her first-born sitting his exams. She was called away to speak to her son on the phone and on returning talked of how he was nervous but thought 'he'd get on all right' and then turned to Mary Wilson, the Prime Minister's wife, commenting, 'You and I would never have got into university.'

Prince Charles did go to university, to Cambridge, after the Queen and her husband sought advice from an eminent gathering that included Harold Wilson, the Archbishop of Canterbury, the Chairman of the Committee of University of Vice-Chancellors and Lord Mountbatten, all of whom were invited to dinner at Buckingham Palace to discuss the education of the heir to the throne.

He read history, but also spent a term at Aberystwyth in 1969 in order to learn the Welsh language.

The Queen's Diamond Jubilee 91

THE 1960s

Charles was invested as Prince of Wales at Caernarfon Castle on 1 July 1969 in a ceremony that had its roots in the medieval age but had been revived again in 1911, in an effort by David Lloyd George to win Liberal votes in the valleys.

Famous for the future King Edward VIII being subjected to wearing – in his own words – a 'preposterous rig' for the occasion, the 1969 ceremony would harness the power of television – an ancient ritual beamed into the country's living rooms through modern technology. The artistic eye of Lord Snowdon, who was Constable of Caernarfon Castle, was called upon to create a stage set for the event and he designed a camera-friendly canopy of Perspex etched with the Prince of Wales feathers.

The investiture turned out to be a great success, with huge television audiences and despite (or perhaps because of) the solemnity of the occasion, the Queen later admitted during a lunch with her mother and Noël Coward that both she and her heir had struggled to stifle their giggles 'because at the dress rehearsal the crown was too big and extinguished him like a candle snuffer!' It is a touching snapshot of a mother and son relationship that could be entirely natural in highly unnatural circumstances.

CHAPTER 4

The Queen's Diamond Jubilee

THE 1960s

The number of royal residents at Buckingham Palace increased by one towards the end of the decade when Princess Alice of Greece, the Duke of Edinburgh's mother, went to live with them following a coup in April 1967 that deposed the Greek royal family.

Disappointingly, her rather eccentric presence was not featured in *Royal Family*. Maybe her nun's habit and chain-smoking were deemed a little too exotic even for 1960s' television audiences or perhaps it was the fact that she still referred to her son (then well into his forties) as 'Bubbikins'.

The Queen got on well with her mother-in-law, while Princes Andrew and Edward, undaunted by their grandmother's imposing appearance or deep, gravelly voice, visited her room frequently. Philip's mother had led an eventful life that included a diagnosis of schizophrenia in 1930 and commitment to a sanatorium, and the founding of a nursing order of Greek Orthodox nuns in 1949.

Her death in 1969, which drew a line under the decade, brought to light a revelation that she had sheltered a Jewish family in Nazi-occupied Athens during the Second World War. She had never spoken of it, but was posthumously awarded the title 'Righteous Among the Nations' at the Holocaust Memorial Centre in Jerusalem in 1993.

For the Queen, the 1960s was a decade of contrasts. At its start, Macmillan had famously told the British they had 'never had it so good' but the good times, permissiveness and prosperity saw the growth of a more cynical, questioning population. As a young queen, Elizabeth II had enjoyed a honeymoon period with the British public but, as they changed, the need for the Crown to modernise and be relevant to the 1960s became ever more apparent.

While the Queen enjoyed a relatively tranquil home life and took pleasure in her growing family, she was faced with often very public criticism of her decisions and actions. She was also forced to concede that an intrusion into a precious portion of her private life was an unavoidable part of regal public relations.

Throughout all this, her sense of duty prevailed and as a woman still in her early forties she did try to move with the times, within the restrictions imposed by her position.

Harold Wilson, a prime minister who really helped shape the period, recommended in 1965 that The Beatles – arguably one of Britain's biggest exports – should individually be awarded the MBE. The Establishment recognising four working-class men from Liverpool (who grew their hair long and played guitars for hordes of screaming girls) was one defining moment in a decade full of them.

Wracked with nerves, the band allegedly smoked marijuana at the palace before accepting their honours. Some previous recipients, feeling that their own award had been devalued, returned their insignia in disgust.

If any one moment was symbolic of the modern monarchy, then this was perhaps it. The Sixties may not have been as swinging for Queen Elizabeth II as it was for her subjects, but she did at least make a discernible effort to sway in time.

96 The Queen's Diamond Jubilee

CHAPTER 5

The 1970s

by ROBERT GOLDEN

EVERY DECADE BRINGS a share of conflicting emotions – births, marriages, deaths and a myriad other occasions affecting family life. But for the Queen and her family these milestones are played out in the glare of public interest and in the spotlight of national, and often international, media reportage. Political events too sometimes influence the Queen's movements, causing unplanned changes to her schedule.

The 1970s were a time of family joy, mourning and celebration for Her Majesty: in 1972 the Queen and the Duke of Edinburgh celebrated their Silver Wedding anniversary, and five years later her Silver Jubilee festivities went on for much of 1977. The weddings of Princess Anne to Captain Mark Phillips, Prince Richard of Gloucester to Miss Birgitte van Deurs, and Prince Michael of Kent to Baroness Marie Christine von Reibnitz were joyous occasions for the wider family. The Queen lost her two remaining uncles, the Dukes of Windsor and Gloucester, both sons of King George V and Queen Mary. Her cousin, Lady Patricia Ramsay, the penultimate surviving grandchild of Queen Victoria, died, and there were the tragic, untimely deaths of Prince William of Gloucester and Earl Mountbatten of Burma.

On the plus side was the birth of the Queen's first grandchild, Peter Phillips, at St Mary's Hospital, Paddington, in November 1977.

THE 1970s

There was also the high-profile separation, followed by divorce in 1978, of Princess Margaret and the Earl of Snowdon. The Queen's first cousin, the Honourable Gerald Lascelles (younger son of the late Princess Royal), who caused a scandal by having a child out of wedlock, was also divorced from his wife Angela in the same year.

The decade began with the Queen and her immediate family welcoming in the new year at Sandringham. They had emerged from a short period of family mourning, the Grim Reaper having worked overtime taking Prince Philip's mother, Princess Alice of Greece, and the Queen's cousin, Lady Helena Gibbs, in December 1969. 'The Firm' was still riding the crest of a wave, much goodwill having been generated the previous summer with the screening of the film *Royal Family*.

During Royal Ascot week in 1970 a glittering party was held at Windsor Castle to celebrate the 70th birthdays of Queen Elizabeth the Queen Mother, the Duke of Gloucester, Earl Mountbatten of Burma and the Duke of Beaufort. Due to an oversight, Sir Henry Abel Smith (the son-in-law of Princess Alice, Countess of Athlone), also 70 that year, was left off the list. Gloucester, by then disabled after a series of strokes, was unable to attend. The presence of one guest was the cause of much criticism in Gibraltar. Prince Juan Carlos, King Designate of Spain, accepted an invitation despite General Franco having closed the border between the Rock and Spain.

That same year the 50-year-old Marquess of Milford Haven, first cousin to Prince Philip and best man at his wedding, collapsed and died at London's Liverpool Street Station, leaving a young wife and two children. The more staid members of the royal family considered the twice-married Marquess rather racy. The Queen was not present at his funeral or at the memorial service at the Queen's Chapel, St James's Palace. Philip attended the latter.

CHAPTER 5

The Queen's Diamond Jubilee 99

THE 1970s

The Duke of Edinburgh predicted that the royal finances would 'go into the red' in 1970. He made this potentially explosive statement during a live interview on NBC television. 'I don't know; we may have to move into smaller premises,' he said. 'We had a small yacht we had to sell, and I shall probably have to give up polo fairly soon.' He opened up a can of worms. Courtiers and the government were highly embarrassed; it is not known what the Queen's reaction was. A Parliamentary Select Committee was set up to examine the royal finances with a view to increasing the Civil List. That well-known scourge of the royal family, the Labour MP Willie Hamilton, described it as 'the most brazenly insensitive pay claim made in the last 200 years'.

The committee scrutinised the expenditure of the royal family in minute detail. Both Princess Margaret and the Duke of Gloucester were heavily criticised. Margaret, the committee observed, had carried out only 31 engagements outside London the previous year. Since she had a working husband and her official duties appeared to be 'extremely limited in number, scope and importance', it was suggested her annuity be cancelled and that free housing was sufficient recompense.

Of the Duke of Gloucester, in receipt of an annual grant of £35,000 since 1937, the committee found that he '…and his family are very remote from the Throne; no evidence was produced as to the amount of public work engaged in over the last 19 years'. It was therefore recommended that the allowance be discontinued.

Yearly payments of £10,000 each to Princes Andrew and Edward, both still children, were described as 'indefensible'. The arguments rumbled on until 1972, when the Conservative majority in Parliament ignored sweeping reforms proposed by the Select Committee, increasing the Civil List from £475,000 to £980,000.

CHAPTER 5

The Queen's Diamond Jubilee 101

THE 1970s

The Queen had a fairly uneventful year in 1971; there were no major family milestones and only one state visit to this country by a foreign monarch: King Mohammed Zahir Shah of Afghanistan visited London from 7-10 December. Less than two years later, he was deposed by his cousin, who declared himself president. Mohammed went into exile in Rome.

Elizabeth and Philip visited Turkey from 18 to 25 October; they also undertook one visit to a Commonwealth country when they toured the Canadian province of British Columbia.

The following year was one of three funerals and a wedding. And a Silver Wedding anniversary too.

By May 1972 it had become known that the Duke of Windsor was dying from throat cancer. After protracted negotiations, it was arranged that the Queen, while on a state visit to Paris, would call on her uncle and aunt at their home in the Bois de Boulogne on her way back from an afternoon of racing at Longchamps. Whilst the Duchess entertained the Duke of Edinburgh and the Prince of Wales to tea, the Queen went to her uncle David's bedroom for a poignant last meeting with him. Despite being connected to various tubes the Duke insisted on being dressed and stood to greet his niece and monarch. As the Queen left, the Duke's doctor noticed that she was fighting back tears.

Nine days later the Duke of Windsor died and his body was flown to RAF Benson, in the Oxfordshire countryside, where it rested overnight in the base chapel. Early the next day it was driven to Windsor Castle for a lying-in-state at St George's Chapel prior to burial at Frogmore. One vigilant press photographer recorded the hearse bearing the Duke's coffin, covered by a royal standard, being driven along a deserted Windsor High Street, passing the formidable-looking statue of his great-grandmother Queen Victoria as it turned to enter the castle's Henry VIII Gate.

CHAPTER 5

The Queen's Diamond Jubilee 103

THE 1970s

On a wet July day the wedding of Elizabeth's cousin, Prince Richard of Gloucester, to Miss Birgitte van Deurs was solemnised in the village church at Barnwell, Northamptonshire, a few hundred yards from the Gloucesters' country estate. His bride was the first Dane to marry into the royal family since Princess Alexandra became the wife of Edward, Prince of Wales in 1863. The Queen and Prince Philip, who were in Scotland on official duties, did not attend (there was also a desire on the part of the bride and bridegroom for a low-key ceremony), but Queen Elizabeth the Queen Mother and the Prince of Wales were among 10 members of the royal family present.

The following month Richard's best man, his elder brother Prince William of Gloucester, was killed whilst flying a Cherokee single-engine aircraft at the Goodyear air race near Wolverhampton. Handsome, debonair and the first royal career diplomat, his postings included Lagos and Tokyo; the 30-year-old Prince had resigned from the Civil Service in 1970 to concentrate on farming the Barnwell estate.

The Queen, who was particularly fond of her cousin and admired his independent spirit, flew down from her summer holiday at Balmoral to attend his funeral at Windsor. Prince Philip and Princess Anne interrupted their official attendance at the Olympic Games in Munich to join her.

The third funeral that year, which again took place at St George's Chapel followed by burial at Frogmore, was that of 91-year-old Sir Alexander Ramsay, husband of the former Princess Patricia of Connaught. His widow, who attended the service in a wheelchair, would follow her husband to the grave 15 months later. For Lady Patricia's funeral the Queen came back early from her winter stay at Sandringham and, with Patricia's niece, Queen Ingrid of Denmark, she followed the coffin, borne by members of Princess Patricia's Canadian Light Infantry, as it left the chapel.

Amongst the important official engagements in 1972, the Queen hosted two royal state visits to the United Kingdom. In April she welcomed Queen Juliana of the Netherlands, followed two months later by Grand Duke Jean of Luxembourg and his wife Joséphine-Charlotte. The Queen and the Duke of Edinburgh undertook four overseas tours, namely Thailand, the Maldives, France and Yugoslavia.

On 20 November the Queen and Prince Philip were present at Westminster Abbey for a service of thanksgiving to mark the 25th anniversary of their marriage. They were joined by their extended family, which included Philip's two surviving sisters: Princess Margarita of Hohenlohe-Langenburg and Princess George of Hanover. The King and Queen of the Hellenes, the Grand Duke and Grand Duchess of Luxembourg, and the Prince and Princess of Liechtenstein were among others present. One hundred couples married on the same day were also invited.

Buckingham Palace announced that the day was to be regarded as a family occasion, rather than a state one; the public had to wait until 1977 for the Silver Jubilee, which would enjoy the panoply of a full state ceremony. Because of this the Queen and her family drove to and from the abbey in motorcars, but later that day a carriage conveyed Elizabeth, Philip and their two elder children from the palace to Guildhall for a formal luncheon.

It was on this occasion that the Queen gave one of her most memorable speeches: 'I think that everybody really will agree that on this, of all days, I should begin my speech with the words "My Husband And I".' Later that day the royal party spent nearly an hour walking to the site of the Barbican development, stopping frequently to talk to the assembled crowds. It was described as the first royal walkabout in London.

On the family front, 1973 was considerably happier than the previous year. Princess Alice, Countess of Athlone celebrated her 90th birthday with a party at the Turf Club. Three queens were present: Elizabeth II, Elizabeth the Queen Mother, and Juliana of the Netherlands. 'Tiaras if possible', the invitation requested. Tiaras there were in abundance; it was truly a glittering occasion.

November saw the marriage of Princess Anne and Captain Mark Phillips at Westminster Abbey. The couple were passionate about equestrian sports, and it is thought that Anne was attracted to Mark because of his prowess in the saddle. The Queen is said to have remarked that she wouldn't be surprised if their children were four-legged. It was announced from Buckingham Palace that Captain Phillips would not receive a title upon his marriage. Both he and Princess Anne did not wish to encumber any children with titles: their offspring would lead private lives, even though their grandmother was the Queen, it was stated.

CHAPTER 5

The Queen's Diamond Jubilee 105

THE 1970s

Whilst on a tour of Australia in October 1973, Elizabeth II opened Sydney Opera House; she also signed the Royal Styles and Titles Bill, which declared that when in Australia she would be known as 'Queen of Australia', with no reference made to her being 'Queen of the United Kingdom and of Her Other Realms and Territories'.

Elizabeth and Philip were back in Australia in February 1974, but her visit was cut short when she had to return to London for a snap General Election. Prince Philip continued the tour alone.

The Queen and the Duke of Edinburgh were on a state visit to Indonesia the following month when early one morning they received a phone call from Princess Anne to tell them about an incident she had been involved in back in London.

On 20 March the Princess and Captain Phillips, together with her lady-in-waiting Rowena Brassey, were returning from a Riding for the Disabled charity event in the City of London, but as they were being driven along The Mall towards Buckingham Palace at around 7.30pm a Ford Escort swerved just in front of their car, forcing it to stop.

A man leapt out and fired a gun at the royal car. Inspector James Beaton, the Princess's protection officer, also got out but almost immediately was shot in the chest. The man, later identified as 26-year-old Ian Ball, then opened the car door and tried to pull Anne out, but her husband managed to drag her back inside the vehicle and slam the door shut.

CHAPTER 5

The Queen's Diamond Jubilee 107

THE 1970s

Using a second gun, Ball proceeded to shoot Beaton again, this time in the hand and stomach. A dialogue between Ball and the Princess ensued in which it became clear that he expected a ransom of three million pounds. Next to be injured was her chauffeur, Alexander Callender, who was shot in the chest at point-blank range, followed by a policeman on duty at nearby St James's Palace who had run across to see what was going on. And then it was the turn of Fleet Street journalist Brian McConnell, who was in a taxi behind the royal car but went to try to resolve the situation.

By this time police were arriving from every direction, and Ball ran into St James's Park to try to escape but was quickly brought down by a rugby tackle from an unarmed detective. It was a miracle that no one was killed. When Ball appeared in court he pleased guilty to attempted kidnapping, attempted murder and wounding, and was sent to Broadmoor Hospital under the Mental Health Act. He is still there. Royal security, until then fairly low key, was tightened significantly thereafter.

On 10 June the Queen's last surviving uncle, Prince Henry, Duke of Gloucester, died at Barnwell Manor after a long debilitating illness. He was 74. Henry was a reluctant royal; never really at home in the limelight, he much preferred the officers' mess or working on his farm. Following his long service in the Army he became Governor-General of Australia.

CHAPTER 5

For his final eight years he was confined to a wheelchair; although communication was impossible, he could understand what was being said to him. When told by his wife, Alice, that their son William had been killed, she knew by his reaction that he had understood. At his funeral at Windsor, his body was conveyed by gun carriage, with full military honours, from Victoria Barracks to St George's Chapel, where the Queen and over a score of royal mourners attended his service.

The Queen has always taken her role as Head of the Commonwealth extremely seriously, enjoying visits to 'Her Other Realms and Territories' enormously. Because she has no desire to interfere with the politics or smooth running of the Commonwealth countries, she was saddened in 1975 when, in her name, the Governor-General of Australia, Sir John Kerr, sacked the Prime Minister, Gough Whitlam, an able and highly popular politician. The Senate, an elected version of the British House of Lords, would not pass the budget proposed by the House of Representatives, thus making it virtually impossible for the country to operate. By sacking an elected Prime Minister and asking the Leader of the Opposition to take over, the Governor-General drew the Queen into a constitutional crisis, the legacy of which still rumbles on even now. Due to the time difference between Britain and Australia, the Palace was not aware of the actions of Sir John Kerr until they were a *fait accompli*.

The Queen's Diamond Jubilee

THE 1970s

Up until that time, it was thought that an ideal job for the Prince of Wales would be to make him Governor-General; following the Kerr debacle, any likelihood of that happening evaporated overnight. The wounds were still fresh when the Queen visited Australia in March 1977. In rural parts of the country she was received enthusiastically, but in Sydney things did not always run smoothly. There were loyal crowds, especially around the harbour area where the Royal Yacht *Britannia* was berthed. Elsewhere the Queen encountered a less than friendly reception. Driving slowly along Macquarie Street on her way to Government House, she was jeered and placards were thrown in the direction of her state motorcar.

Elizabeth got on very well with her fifth British Prime Minister, Harold Wilson; when he retired due to failing health in 1976, she and Philip attended his farewell dinner at 10 Downing Street. This was the highest compliment that she could pay to her outgoing first officer – the last time she had visited the Prime Minister's official residence was for Sir Winston Churchill's retirement dinner in 1955.

Her Majesty passed a personal milestone on 21 April 1976 when she reached the age of 50. The day was spent quietly at Windsor, as she did not want a fuss or any public expenditure on what she regarded as a private family occasion. Her only engagement was to hold a tea party for 180 members of the Victoria

Cross and George Cross Association. The previous evening the Queen gave a dinner for 50 close friends and family, followed by a ball for 500 guests. This birthday occurred on a Wednesday, the same day that she was born.

Interestingly, on 21 April 1926 King George V and Queen Mary had given lunch at Windsor to Princess Alice of Greece – Prince Philip's mother – and the Dowager Marchioness of Milford Haven, his grandmother.

In the summer of 1976 the Queen, Prince Philip and their four children attended the Olympic Games in Montreal as part of a 13-day tour of Canada. The royal couple had come from the United States, where they attended celebrations marking the bicentenary of the Declaration of Independence. At a banquet in Philadelphia the Queen was exposed to the somewhat bizarre behaviour of the Mayor, Frank Rizzo. Seated next to him for dinner, she was amused that he frequently left the table to 'glad-hand' guests seated at other tables. Her Majesty, with her usual *sang-froid*, took it entirely in her stride, but her two ladies-in-waiting were furious.

Early that year the monarch had been saddened by the decision of Princess Margaret and Lord Snowdon to separate. A terse statement from Kensington Palace on 19 March 1976 informed the world of the breakdown of the marriage: 'HRH The Princess Margaret, Countess of Snowdon, and the Earl of Snowdon have mutually agreed to live apart. The Princess will carry out her public duties unaccompanied by Lord Snowdon. There are no plans for divorce proceedings.'

Divorce, however, did follow two years later. On a more positive note, the Queen bought the 730-acre Gatcombe Park estate for Princess Anne and Captain Phillips; she was reported to have paid in the region of £300,000 for the house, grounds and stables.

Several Labour MPs were outraged. Dennis Skinner, MP for Bolsover, recalled that the previous year the Commons were told the royal family was 'on the verge of bankruptcy'. 'Hundreds of MPs were lured into the voting lobby to increase the substantial holdings of the royal family,' he opined. 'Now the truth is out.'

THE 1970s

During 1976 the lease on Fort Belvedere, an 18th-century Crown property in Windsor Great Park, the former home of King Edward VIII (where he signed the Instrument of Abdication in 1936), was sold by his nephew, the Honourable Gerald Lascelles, for £200,000. Mr Lascelles, who was living apart from his wife Angela, had bought it in 1955. He was now living with Elizabeth Collingwood, who would become his second wife, and by whom he already had a son. Again the Queen was horrified and embarrassed by the lack of moral fibre of some of her not-too-distant relations.

Another cause for concern that year was when Princess Alexandra, the Queen's first cousin, received Communion at a service at the Vatican. The Princess was attending the canonisation of Blessed John Ogilvie, an ancestor of the Princess's husband, Angus Ogilvy, at St Peter's Basilica. It was explained that she had received Communion 'out of politeness, and was unaware of the Catholic ruling that non-Catholics should not partake'. This did not prevent an Italian newspaper, *La Stampa*, from accusing her of causing an 'ecumenical scandal'. It was thought to be the first time since the Reformation that a member of the royal family had received Communion in a Roman Catholic church.

CHAPTER 5

The portents for the Queen's Silver Jubilee in 1977 were not promising. Britain was suffering economically: inflation had hit 16 per cent, there was widespread unemployment, and there were swingeing cuts in public expenditure. Quite naturally, Elizabeth did not wish to add to the financial burden that would be imposed if the government and local authorities organised extravagant celebrations.

She need not have worried; the United Kingdom was soon in a celebratory mood. Not since the Coronation had such a spontaneous, feel-good atmosphere existed throughout the British peoples.

The Queen was flabbergasted by the welcome she received wherever she went. She felt truly humbled by the warmth and interest shown in her whilst travelling over 56,000 miles during her British and Commonwealth progress.

The Silver Jubilee visits started early in the year, when on 9 February the Queen and Prince Philip left for a tour of some Commonwealth countries. They flew to Samoa, then visited Tonga, Fiji, New Zealand, Australia, Papua-New Guinea and Australia again; finally returning to London on 31 March.

During May she was in Scotland for 10 days, where in Edinburgh she attended the opening session of the General Assembly of the Church of Scotland. This was followed by a Beating Retreat ceremony and a state banquet, both at the Palace of Holyroodhouse. At the end of the month Elizabeth II was present at a gala performance at the Royal Opera House, Covent Garden.

The Queen's Diamond Jubilee 113

THE 1970s

The centrepiece of the celebrations was a service of thanksgiving at St Paul's Cathedral. Elizabeth travelled to the cathedral in the Gold State Coach, last used at her Coronation. The service was attended by 34 members of the royal family, the oldest being 94-year-old Princess Alice, Countess of Athlone, who aged 14 had taken part in the Diamond Jubilee procession of her grandmother Queen Victoria in 1897. The youngest participant was Lord Nicholas Windsor, second son of the Duke and Duchess of Kent, who celebrated his seventh birthday the following month. Prince Philip's two surviving sisters, and many of the Queen's Bowes Lyon relations had prominent seats in St Paul's.

Afterwards, the Queen walked to Guildhall, through streets thronged with cheering crowds, for a luncheon given by the Lord Mayor of London for 650 guests.

Other highlights of the year were visits to most of the British Isles (Northern Ireland included, despite security concerns), a naval review at Spithead, off Portsmouth, and ceremonial drives through London boroughs. During a visit to Leeds in July, Elizabeth had a public reconciliation with her cousin, the Earl of Harewood and his second wife, Patricia. Although they had attended the St Paul's service, they were not seated with the royal family but were several rows behind. The Queen had not approved of him having a child out of wedlock by Patricia whilst still married to his first wife, Marion. For several years he was banished from family occasions; most notably he was not invited to the funeral of the Duke of Windsor or the wedding of Princess Anne. However, he and his wife had been present at the Duke of Gloucester's funeral.

The Silver Jubilee celebrations ended with an 18-day tour of Canada, the Bahamas, the Virgin Islands, Antigua, and Barbados. The Queen returned to London on Concorde.

Elizabeth was in celebratory mood on 15 November 1977 when her first grandchild, Peter Phillips, was born at St Mary's Hospital in west London. Her Majesty received the news just before an investiture at Buckingham Palace. Arriving in the Throne Room ten minutes late, she told the waiting audience: 'I have just had a message from the hospital. My daughter has given birth to a son, and I am now a grandmother.'

CHAPTER 5

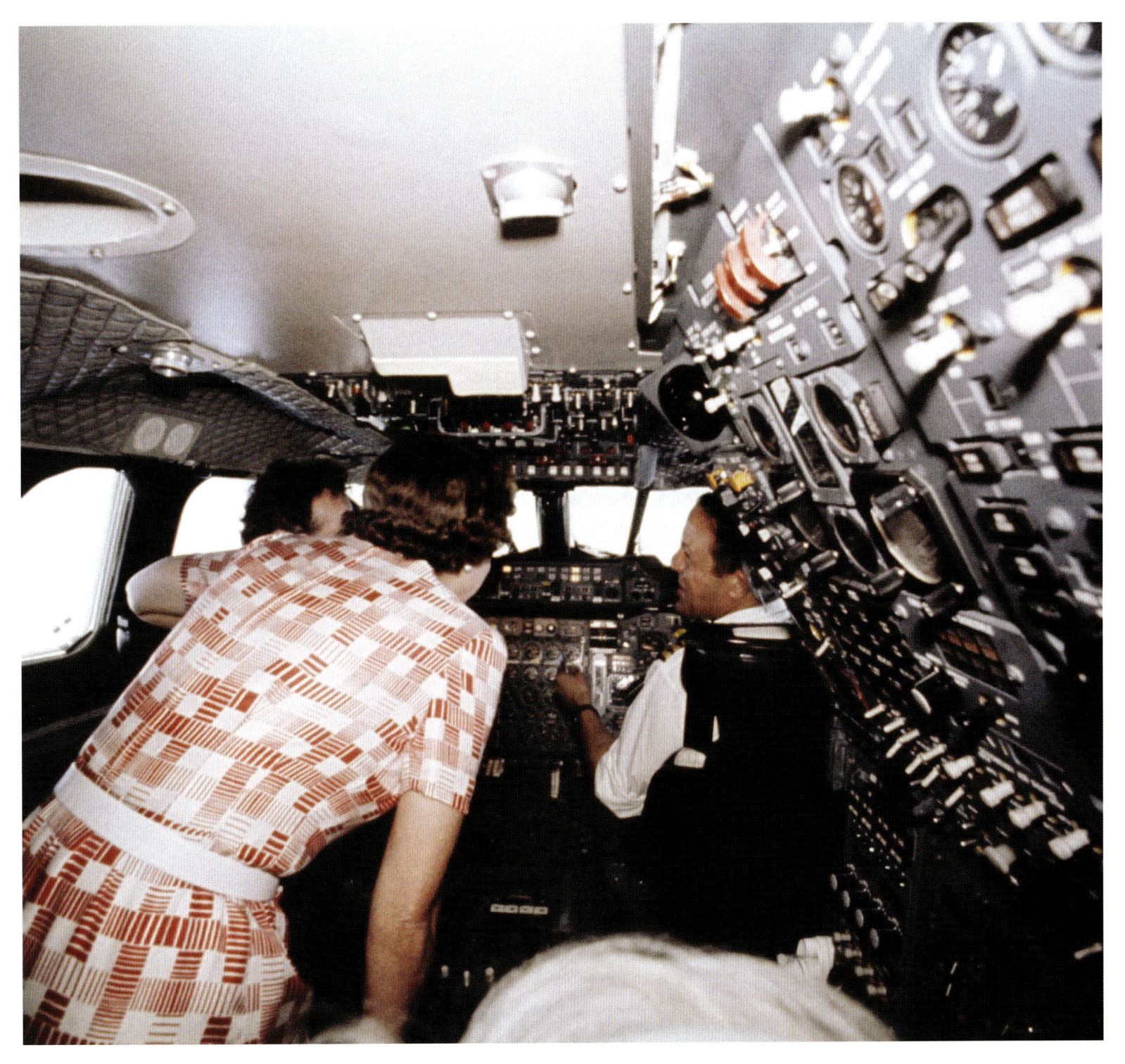

The Queen's Diamond Jubilee 115

THE 1970s

For three days in June 1978 the Queen was obliged to entertain President Ceausescu of Romania and his wife when they stayed at Buckingham Palace for a state visit. The couple, used to the cloak-and-dagger life of a hardened communist regime, were certain that their rooms had been bugged; consequently, whenever they wanted to talk privately they would disappear into the garden. The Queen found them odd and unpredictable. The presidential pair caused consternation and embarrassment by spending enormous amounts of money on luxury goods, leaving the British government to pick up the bill.

The General Election that year saw the appointment of Britain's first female Prime Minister in the form of Margaret Hilda Thatcher – the first time the two highest constitutional roles were occupied by women.

Prince Michael of Kent, another first cousin of the Queen, married Baroness Marie Christine Agnes Hedwig Ida von Reibnitz, the daughter of a German baron and a Hungarian countess, at the Rathaus in Vienna on 30 June.

Because Marie Christine was a Roman Catholic, Prince Michael lost his place in the order of succession to the throne; at the time it was thought that the Marriages Act of 1836 prevented members of the royal family marrying in a registry office in England, hence the Austrian nuptials. (This proved not to be the case when the Prince of Wales and Camilla Parker Bowles married in a civil ceremony at the Guildhall in Windsor in April 2005). The Queen did not attend the Kent wedding, but later that year she gave a family party for the couple at St James's Palace.

116 The Queen's Diamond Jubilee

CHAPTER 5

The Queen's Diamond Jubilee 117

THE 1970s

August has sometimes been a month of tragic deaths for the Queen and royal family, Prince William of Gloucester being killed on Bank Holiday Monday 1972 and, of course, Diana, Princess of Wales on 31 August 1997. Another Bank Holiday Monday, 27 August 1979, saw the assassination of Admiral of the Fleet The Earl Mountbatten of Burma by the Provisional IRA.

Mountbatten had been enjoying his customary summer holiday at Classiebawn Castle, his home in County Sligo, which was a mere 12 miles from the border with Northern Ireland. He was to spend the day lobster fishing with his elder daughter Patricia, her husband Lord Brabourne, their twin sons Nicholas and Timothy Knatchbull, Brabourne's mother, the Dowager Lady Brabourne, and the 15-year-old boatman, Paul Maxwell. A bomb attached to the underside of the boat was detonated by remote control when the party was just outside Mullaghmore Harbour, killing Mountbatten, Nicholas and Paul. The 82-year-old dowager died in Sligo Hospital the following day from shock. John and Patricia Brabourne, and their son Timothy, who miraculously survived the blast, spent several weeks in hospital recovering from their wounds.

Dickie Mountbatten's body, along with those of his grandson and the Dowager Lady Brabourne, was flown to Southampton to be met by Prince Philip and Prince Charles. The remains were transported to his country seat, Broadlands. There was a day's lying-in-state at Romsey Abbey before Mountbatten's body was taken to London, where it rested overnight in the Queen's Chapel at St James's Palace.

Earl Mountbatten of Burma had planned his funeral with military precision, deciding which detachments of British and foreign troops would precede the gun carriage on its journey from the chapel to Westminster Abbey.

Five princes followed the coffin along the route: Philip, Duke of Edinburgh; Charles, Prince of Wales; Richard, Duke of Gloucester; Edward, Duke of Kent; and Prince Michael of Kent.

Inside the abbey, as well as Mountbatten's own family there were gathered 28 members of the royal family, five European reigning heads of state, and four former sovereigns.

After the service his remains were taken by armoured car to Waterloo Station, from where the Queen, Prince Philip and other mourners travelled by special train to Romsey for the interment in the abbey.

Later that day a reception was held at Broadlands. Among the guests was Lady Iris Mountbatten, a member of the royal family, who had lived in North America for over 30 years, rarely visiting England. Apart from the Mountbattens and the Queen, who said a few kind words to her, no one else appeared to know who she was.

Although the decade did have some low points for the Queen, they were minor compared to the family upheavals she would experience 20 years on. The 1970s were mainly a period when the royal family was still treated with respect and some affection.

118 The Queen's Diamond Jubilee

CHAPTER 5

The Queen's Diamond Jubilee 119

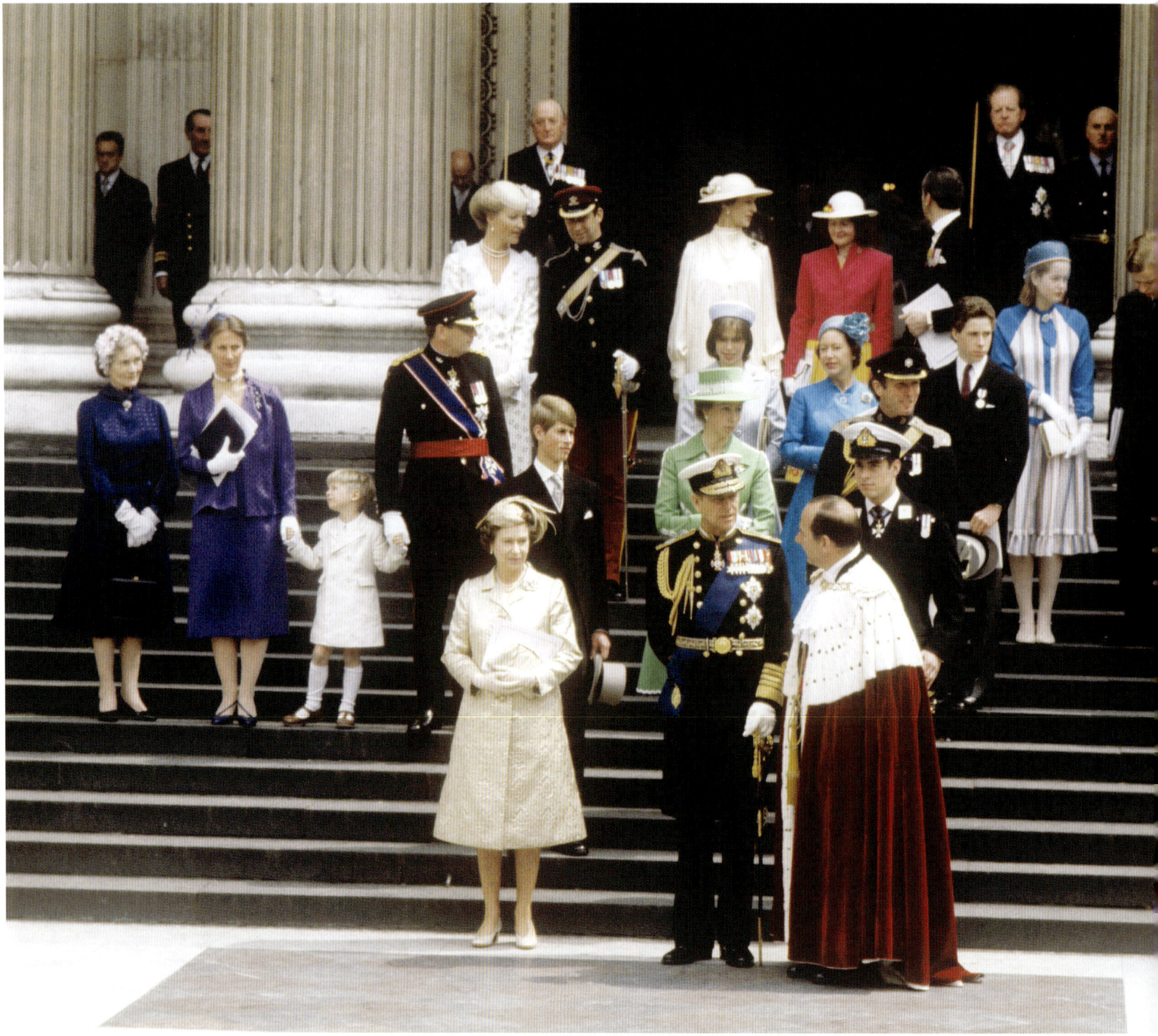

CHAPTER 6

The 1980s

by IAN LLOYD

THE 1980S WERE perceived at the time to be a period of relative peace and stability for the Queen and her relations, though we now know this was far from true. Behind the public image of a happy, united family was the unhappy truth that the marriages of two of the monarch's children were in serious difficulty by the end of the decade.

Her Majesty was now in her mid-fifties, and inevitably much of the focus henceforth would be on the younger generation. Her eldest son, the Prince of Wales, would marry Lady Diana Spencer in 1981, and five years later Prince Andrew would wed Sarah Ferguson. Four of the Queen's eight grandchildren – Zara Phillips, Princes William and Harry and Princess Beatrice – were born during these years.

Media coverage of such events was almost unanimously positive, but by the end of the decade criticism of the less than regal antics of some of the monarch's children and their spouses began to be voiced. By the late 1980s newspapers were to become increasingly obsessed with the state of Charles and Diana's marriage, with the Queen, angered by Fleet Street's worst excesses, resorting to suing tabloids on several occasions.

The decade began with Queen Elizabeth the Queen Mother's 80th birthday celebrations, the first major royal event since the Silver Jubilee three years earlier. Widowed at the age of 51, Queen Elizabeth had chosen not to fade into the background as some queens dowager had done; instead, she played a full and vibrant part in royal life and was as popular as her elder daughter – if not more so – thanks to her skill at public relations and her evident ease when meeting people from all walks of life.

Early in her reign, Queen Elizabeth II is reported to have looked from a palace window at the crowds milling outside and said: 'If I were Mummy, I'd be down there with them now.'

The Queen's Diamond Jubilee 121

THE 1980s

Lady Pamela Mountbatten, who acted as lady-in-waiting on the 1953-4 tour of the Commonwealth, recalled that the new monarch felt the people would not respond to her as they would to her mother, and she was surprised at the positive reaction the tour received. Through the ensuing decades the Queen never took the public's affection for granted and even now is taken aback by the warmth of the crowds that appear at royal weddings, jubilees and landmark birthdays. But her mother never had any doubts about her own popularity and embraced the public celebrations of her 80th birthday with gusto.

The crowds along The Mall were reportedly ten deep when, on 15 July 1980, the Queen Mother and Prince Charles set off from Buckingham Palace in the 1902 State Landau to St Paul's Cathedral for a service of thanksgiving. For once the Queen ceded to her mother the monarch's right to be last to arrive and first to leave. She would do the same that afternoon at a Buckingham Palace balcony appearance and later at a Covent Garden gala attended by most of the royal family, when the Queen and Princess Margaret followed their mother into the royal box as meekly as they would have done as girls some 40 years earlier.

The Queen Mother's actual birthday was 4 August, and this engendered another outpouring of public affection as crowds flocked to see her make her customary birthday appearance at the gates of Clarence House. Queen Elizabeth made few concessions to her age during the 1980s and undertook regular overseas tours, her final one being to Canada in July 1989 when she was a few weeks short of her 89th birthday.

CHAPTER 6

That same summer, attention turned from the previous Queen Consort to a potential future one, when Lady Diana Spencer was rumoured to be dating Prince Charles. Years earlier, the Prince had said that he felt 30 was the right age to marry, and not surprisingly by the late 1970s his love life was a constant theme in the press.

It gave rise to a new breed of journalist – the freelance photographer – who, rather than being employed by one newspaper, could tout his or her wares to the highest bidder in the United Kingdom and around the world.

Prince Charles, the world's most eligible bachelor, didn't disappoint and gave them a never-ending supply of girlfriends, from the Duke of Wellington's daughter Lady Jane Wellesley to Diana's elder sister, Lady Sarah Spencer.

Diana had been spotted with Charles at Cowes Regatta and had also been seen watching him play polo at Midhurst in Sussex earlier in the summer. But it was when she was photographed watching him fish in the River Dee on the Balmoral estate that she was catapulted into the spotlight. Fleet Street was well aware that meeting the Queen at this most private of residences was regarded as the litmus test for acceptance into the royal family.

Although happy to welcome Diana into 'The Firm', Her Majesty was less enamoured about the media frenzy that began after news of the relationship broke in September 1980. Three months later, Diana's mother, Mrs Frances Shand Kydd, complained of the constant press harassment of her daughter, and the Queen was livid that her Christmas and New Year break at Sandringham was ruined by having to continually run the gauntlet of telephoto lenses all over her Norfolk estate.

The Queen's Diamond Jubilee 123

THE 1980s

124 The Queen's Diamond Jubilee

CHAPTER 6

It was while she was staying in East Anglia that winter that the Queen received the news of the death of her great-aunt Princess Alice, Countess of Athlone, at the age of 97 – a record for royal longevity that would last until the Queen Mother's death at the age of 101. 'Aunt Alice' was Queen Victoria's last surviving granddaughter and was a particular favourite of the present Queen. On her final visit to see the feisty old lady, by then bed-ridden in her apartment at Kensington Palace, the monarch was amused when Alice urged her to turn the electric fire off on her way out. 'They only put it on because you were coming,' she explained.

Seven weeks after the death of the oldest Princess, Britain geared itself up to meet its newest one, when the engagement of Charles and Diana was announced on 24 February 1981. A Buckingham Palace statement said simply: 'It is with the greatest pleasure that the Queen and the Duke of Edinburgh announce the betrothal of their beloved son, the Prince of Wales, to Lady Diana Spencer, daughter of the Earl Spencer and the Honourable Mrs Shand Kydd.'

A month later the Queen gave her formal consent to the marriage at a meeting of the Privy Council and afterwards posed for photographs with her 32-year-old son and his shy fiancée.

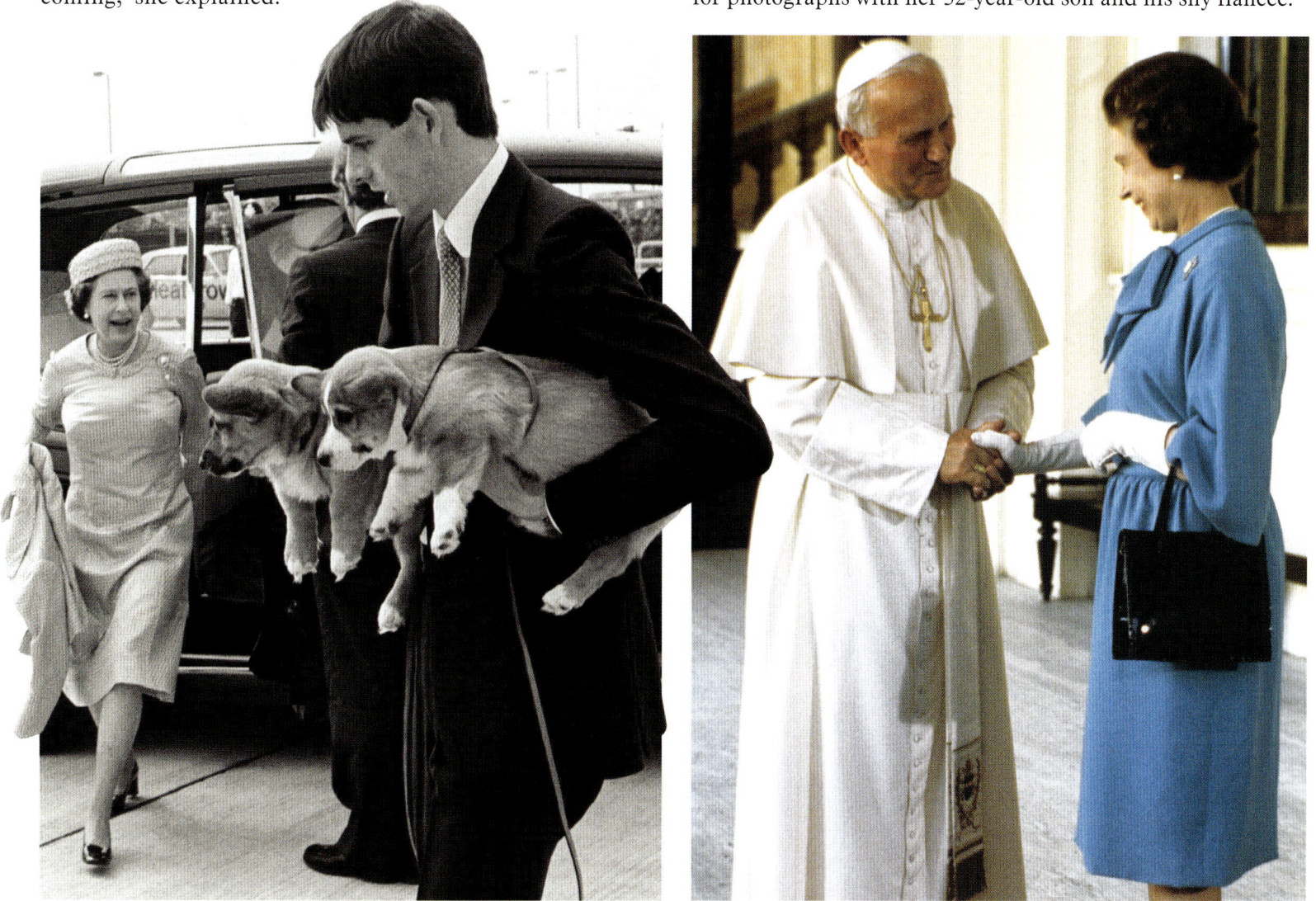

The Queen's Diamond Jubilee 125

THE 1980s

On 15 May the Queen became a grandmother for the second time when Princess Anne gave birth to a daughter in the Lindo wing of St Mary's Hospital, Paddington. The baby, then sixth in line to the throne, was christened Zara Anne Elizabeth at a private ceremony at Windsor Castle on 27 July, two days before the royal wedding.

A record worldwide TV audience of 750 million was reckoned to have tuned in to see Charles and Diana marry at St Paul's Cathedral, in a break with the 20th-century tradition of favouring Westminster Abbey. It was deemed a state occasion and nearly every crowned head of Europe was present, as were many world leaders. As she emerged from the Glass Coach on to the steps of St Paul's, Diana gave the world its first glimpse of the cream silk gown designed by David and Elizabeth Emanuel with its huge 25ft train created to match the grandeur of the setting. In his address following the exchange of vows, the Archbishop of Canterbury, Robert Runcie, memorably said 'this is the stuff of fairytales' – a phrase that would come back to haunt the couple in later years as much as Charles's reply when asked, on the day of his engagement, if he was in love. 'Whatever love means,' was his tortured response.

The royal wedding created a media frenzy that showed no signs of abating for the rest of the year. Following the couple's return from a honeymoon cruise on the Royal Yacht *Britannia* they joined the Queen for a holiday on the Balmoral estate. Diana in particular looked tanned and relaxed at a photocall for over a hundred journalists near the River Dee. She told the press pack she could 'highly recommend' married life.

CHAPTER 6

The Queen's Diamond Jubilee 127

THE 1980s

By the end of the year, however, that other honeymoon – between the royals and Fleet Street – was over. In November it was announced that the Princess of Wales was pregnant, which only intensified media interest in the newlyweds. On 8 December the Queen summoned Fleet Street editors to Buckingham Palace to discuss the persistent press harassment of the royal family – and Diana in particular.

The monarch herself had experienced a much milder form of media intrusion when she and Princess Margaret were young, with photographers always waiting outside London nightclubs and restaurants to snap them. Before their marriage, Prince Philip once took Elizabeth for a spin in his red MG and as they left the palace they were followed by photographers, which the Princess found 'annoying'.

Elizabeth and Margaret were of course born into royal life, unlike 20-year-old Diana, and the Queen was worried about the strain the constant scrutiny was putting on her daughter-in-law. After a briefing by Michael Shea, the Queen's Press Secretary, editors discussed press and palace relations with Her Majesty. While most were sympathetic to the Princess's plight and agreed to review their policy on royal coverage, there was one exception. Shea had complained that photographers had even pursued Diana into the village shop at Tetbury, near the Highgrove estate.

'Wouldn't it be better to send a servant to the shop for Princess Diana's wine gums?' Barry Askew, editor of the *News of the World*, cheekily asked the Queen. 'Mr Askew,' came the icy reply, 'That was a most pompous remark.'

The situation didn't improve. In February 1982 a clearly pregnant Diana was photographed swimming off a private beach in the Bahamas, resulting in a scoop for *The Sun*. The Queen called it 'a black day for British journalism'.

While Her Majesty was sympathetic to Diana's plight with the media, she was unable to instinctively empathise with her daughter-in-law's bulimia and her over-emotional behaviour. She was, however, genuinely shocked to witness Diana throw herself down the stairs at Sandringham, though neither the Princess nor her unborn child was hurt.

The Queen became a grandmother for the third time on 21 June 1982, when Diana gave birth to Prince William at St Mary's Hospital, Paddington. Publicly she was said by the

Palace to be 'delighted' at the birth. In private, when the 40th monarch since the Norman Conquest met the newborn likely 42nd – all being well – her first words were: 'Well, at least he hasn't got his father's ears!' The baby was christened William Arthur Philip Louis at Buckingham Palace on 4 August, the Queen Mother's 82nd birthday.

Prince William was born exactly a week after Argentine forces surrendered to the British, concluding the 74-day Falklands War. The conflict began on 2 April 1982 when Argentina invaded the Falkland Islands and South Georgia in a dispute over sovereignty. The British Prime Minister, Margaret Thatcher, sent a naval task force to engage with the Argentine Navy and Air Force, and to take back control of the islands by amphibious assault. The war resulted in the deaths of 257 British and 649 Argentine personnel.

THE 1980s

The Queen's concerns were twofold. As head of state – and Head of the Armed Forces – she was briefed constantly about the events in the South Atlantic and broadcast a message to the nation at the start of hostilities. On a more personal level, her 22-year-old son Prince Andrew, a serving helicopter pilot, was on board HMS *Invincible*, which had sailed with the task force.

The Prince played an active part in the fighting. On one occasion he used his helicopter as a decoy for the deadly Exocet missiles fired by Argentinean jets at the British task force vessels. He also witnessed the bombing of the *Atlantic Conveyor* supply ship and was among those who helped to rescue its crew.

130 The Queen's Diamond Jubilee

'It was horrific and terrible and something I'll never forget,' he later revealed. 'It was probably my most frightening moment of the war.'

Andrew arrived back at Portsmouth on 16 September after more than five months away at sea. The Queen, Prince Philip and Princess Anne sailed out to meet *Invincible* for an emotional private reunion.

In her 1982 Christmas broadcast the Queen praised the work of the Royal Navy and the Merchant Navy, which she said displayed: 'the professional skills and courage that could be called on in defence of basic freedoms'.

The historic visits of two heads of state proved a useful diversion for the Queen during the Falklands War. In May, Pope John Paul II paid a pastoral visit to the UK – the first by a Pope to Britain for 450 years – although at one point it looked like it might be postponed because of the war.

During his tour he drove through the gates of Buckingham Palace in his 'Popemobile' before spending over half an hour in talks with the Queen, the Supreme Governor of the Church of England. During his visit the Pope gave her a bas-relief of Christ on the cross, and told his host: 'I will pray for your son in the Falklands.'

THE 1980s

The following month the President of the United States of America and Mrs Reagan stayed with the Queen at Windsor Castle. Her Majesty has scrupulously avoided having favourites among foreign leaders, just as she has treated all her UK prime ministers with impartiality. Having said that, of the 11 US presidents she has met face to face, Ronald Reagan is the only one to have stayed with her at Windsor and, as horse lovers, it was clear they bonded as they went for an early-morning ride in the Home Park.

In 1983 the Reagans returned the favour and invited the Queen and Prince Philip to their ranch in California, a visit made all the more memorable due to the torrential rain that made the royal journey to the mountaintop retreat hazardous. Instead of riding together two couple stayed indoors by a fire stocked with wood the President had cut himself.

A less welcome visit that summer was one made by Michael Fagan, an unemployed north London labourer, who not only managed to break into Buckingham Palace but also then made his way to the Queen's bedroom unimpeded. He spent 10 minutes alone with Her Majesty. The incident happened at 7.15am on 9 July. Fagan woke the Queen, who twice rang the police for help but to no avail.

According to the intruder, she did not seem nervous or worried; when he asked for a cigarette she cleverly used this as an excuse to get him out into the corridor. Here they were confronted by a maid, but at the same point the Queen's page, Paul Whybrew, returned from walking the corgis and kept Fagan occupied by offering him a drink until the police finally arrived on the scene.

The Queen wanted the incident hushed up but the ensuing Home Office investigation was leaked to the press. Fagan himself said royal security was 'diabolical' and the monarch, for one, could hardly disagree.

Newspaper reports focused on it being only a year since another major security alert. On 14 June 1981, 17-year-old Marcus Sergeant fired six blank shots at the Queen as she entered Horse Guards Approach Road before the Trooping the Colour ceremony. Despite riding side-saddle the Queen

132 The Queen's Diamond Jubilee

expertly controlled her horse Burmese, which was startled by the noise. Her main concern was for the welfare of Princes Philip and Charles who were following her, also on horseback. 'I didn't know what was happening,' she said later. That September, Sergeant was found guilty and sent to jail for five years, though he was later committed to a psychiatric hospital.

As the decade progressed, relations with Fleet Street deteriorated. In October 1982, the Queen was dismayed when Prince Andrew was forced to cut short a much-needed break in the West Indies with his girlfriend, the former actress Koo Stark, due to excessive media attention.

The following February, Her Majesty took the unprecedented step of imposing a legal injunction on a former palace servant for revealing royal secrets. This followed revelations in *The Sun* about the alleged behaviour of Prince Andrew and his girlfriend under the headline 'Queen Koo's Romps at the Palace'. The next instalment, 'Barefoot Diana Buttered My Toast', never saw the light of day.

The Queen had met Koo at Balmoral and seemingly wasn't bothered that she had had other boyfriends or had taken part in a soft-porn movie directed by the Earl of Pembroke. But the British press, naturally, revelled in it all, and the constant references to 'former porn star Koo Stark' effectively scuppered the chances of marriage.

In 1987 the Queen once again initiated legal proceedings against *The Sun* for breach of copyright when it published a letter written by the Duke of Edinburgh to the Commandant of the Royal Marines in which he referred to Prince Edward's decision to quit his service career with the unit.

The following year the newspaper agreed to pay £100,000 to charity after publishing a photograph of the Queen and her newborn granddaughter Beatrice taken at Balmoral during the summer. On a more positive note, the 1980s saw both Prince Charles and Princess Anne gain respect for their charity work and for carving out, in their own fields, roles more challenging than the traditional ribbon-cutting way of royal life.

In the autumn of 1982 Princess Anne undertook a gruelling six-nation tour of Africa and the Middle East in her capacity as president of the Save the Children Fund. In the previous decade the Queen's only daughter had been labelled 'Princess Sourpuss' by the press and was famous for her 'Naff Off' stance with photographers. Now Fleet Street's finest were falling over themselves to compliment her on her hands-on approach during a 14,000-mile tour during which she saw starving children in refugee camps in Somalia and visited makeshift hospitals in Beirut and Swaziland.

Two months after the 1985 Live Aid concert helped to raise millions for Africa's starving peoples, Anne made a crusading speech at a conference of 60 Third World countries in Scotland. 'Drought and famine are not new in Africa,' she told them. 'Their effect can be moderated with sensible and basic precautions and planning by everybody.'

In June 1987, Anne finally gave in to pressure from her family and accepted the Queen's offer of the title Princess Royal, which is usually bestowed on the eldest daughter of the sovereign shortly after the death of the previous holder. This time there was a 22-year gap between the death of the Queen's aunt, Princess Mary, in 1965 and Anne's acceptance of the honour.

Prince Charles proved he was no mere figurehead when, in May 1984, he addressed a gathering of leading architects at Hampton Court Palace. He launched an attack on the work of modern architects and in particular those who had submitted plans for the proposed extension of London's National Gallery. He singled out the design by Peter Ahrends as 'a kind of vast municipal fire station… like a monstrous carbuncle on the face of a much-loved and elegant friend'.

The Prince of Wales's speech caused a rumpus in the press and not surprisingly Ahrends condemned the comments as offensive, reactionary and ill considered.

THE 1980s

The following year Prince Charles was involved in further controversy when his concerns that he did not wish to rule over a 'divided Britain' were leaked to the press by a friend, the community architect Rod Hackney. 'He is very worried that when he becomes King there will be 'no-go' areas in the inner cities and that racial minorities will be alienated from the west of the country,' Hackney revealed. This was immediately seized on by Labour MPs as a direct attack on Margaret Thatcher's government.

The Queen has remained admirably neutral when it comes to politics, but in what it called an 'unprecedented disclosure of the monarch's political views', *The Sunday Times* in July 1986 carried the story that she, like her son, was profoundly worried about the direction in which Britain was heading. The newspaper claimed the monarch regarded Mrs Thatcher's radical reforms as 'uncaring, confrontational and divisive', and that they were threatening to undermine 'the consensus in British politics which she thinks has served the country well since the Second World War'.

The source of the leak was discovered to be the Queen's Press Secretary, Michael Shea, who denied Her Majesty had ever said anything along these lines. Her Private Secretary, William Heseltine, fired off a letter to *The Times* in which he stated that it was 'preposterous' that the Queen, after 34 years on the throne, would suddenly abandon her strict rule on unbiased impartiality and attack the government of the day.

July ended on a more positive note when Prince Andrew married Sarah Ferguson in Westminster Abbey. 'Fergie', as the press dubbed her, was widely regarded at the time as the perfect choice for Andrew. She had an impeccable pedigree: not only was she descended from King Charles II but also her maternal grandmother was a cousin of Princess Alice, Duchess of Gloucester. Her father 'Major Ron' was a polo-playing friend of Prince Philip and was Prince Charles's polo manager.

THE 1980s

138 The Queen's Diamond Jubilee

CHAPTER 6

In January 1986 the Queen invited Sarah Ferguson to Sandringham, where the royal family welcomed the bubbly redhead and soon regarded her as a breath of fresh air after the complicated and insecure Diana. Sarah was at ease with country life. She went riding with the Queen, who took to her exuberant, fun-loving personality.

Andrew and Sarah's engagement was announced on 19 March and they were married on 23 July. The Queen created her son Duke of York, a title particularly close to her heart as it had been bestowed on her father in 1920; she herself had been Princess Elizabeth of York. As a belated wedding present, Elizabeth paid the alleged £3.5 million cost of building the couple a dream house at Sunninghill, the other side of Windsor Great Park to Windsor Castle. The sprawling ranch-style house was immediately dubbed 'South York' after the Southfork estate owned by the oil-rich Ewing family in the popular TV show *Dallas*.

While the Queen and her family were preparing for the wedding, the final chapter of another royal romance ended in April 1986 with the death of the Duchess of Windsor at her home on the Bois de Boulogne in Paris. Half a century earlier, Elizabeth's uncle, the besotted King Edward VIII, had abdicated in order to marry the twice-divorced Wallis Simpson, forcing the Queen's reluctant father to succeed to the throne. The Queen Mother never forgave the Windsors, believing the pressures of kingship led to her husband's untimely death.

In the autumn of 1986 the Queen embarked on one of her most memorable tours when, accompanied by the Duke of Edinburgh, she became the first British monarch to visit China. They were taken to the Great Wall, posing for photographs before setting off for a short walk along one of its sections. They also travelled to Xi'an in Shaanxi province to see the Terracotta Army that had been unearthed only 12 years earlier.

The tour was overshadowed by a diplomatic incident when Prince Philip came out with one of his legendary gaffes, telling British students at a reception that he found Beijing 'ghastly' and suggesting that 'if you stay here much longer you'll go back with slitty eyes'. Although Michael Shea insisted: 'Jocular comments have been taken completely out of context', the British press, relishing a good story, nicknamed Philip 'The Great Wally of China'.

While Charles and Anne had prospered during the decade, neither Andrew nor his younger brother Edward captured the public's imagination in the same way. Despite his marriage and the birth of his daughter Beatrice in 1988, Andrew never regained the popularity he richly deserved during the Falklands War.

Andrew's 1984 five-day tour of America was a public relations disaster after he sprayed paint over photographers and their cameras during a visit to a housing estate in Los Angeles. Although he made a belated apology, the Prince was widely believed to have harmed the royal family's image in the United States. One commentator labelled it 'the most unpleasant royal visit since they burnt the White House in 1812'.

Prince Edward's popularity also dipped when he dropped out of the Marines in January 1987. The Prince's resignation, after just four months' training, was a blow to Prince Philip, Captain General of the Marines, and he was said to be furious at his son's decision.

In retrospect, it can be claimed that a more insidiously damaging effect on the monarchy's popularity during these years came from the constant appearances of members of the royal family on television. Princess Anne, the Duke of York and their father appeared on chat shows like *Aspel*, *Wogan* and *Parkinson*; Anne also made a memorable appearance on *A Question of Sport*. Even Princess Margaret, normally a stickler for protocol and tradition, appeared on the BBC radio series *The Archers* playing herself and was also a guest on *Desert Island Discs*.

Royal TV appearances reached their nadir in the summer of 1987 when Prince Edward produced *It's a Royal Knockout*, a charity fundraiser that rapidly turned into another PR disaster. Edward, Andrew, Sarah and, surprisingly, Anne agreed to captain teams of celebrities who competed in a tournament at Alton Towers. To make matters worse, Edward became petulant at a post-production press conference. After asking the media what they thought of the show, which they had to watch on TV monitors, the Prince received a lukewarm response. 'Well, thanks a lot,' he snapped before walking out. Though never made public, the Queen's reaction can easily be guessed.

The Queen's Diamond Jubilee 139

THE 1980s

The decade that started so promisingly for the royal family with the wedding of Charles and Diana ended with their union in tatters, though only a select few were aware that the marriage had reached crisis point by 1986. The public was fed the myth that everything was fine; it would be another six years before the truth exploded on to newspaper front pages.

In October 1985, 20 million UK viewers watched a 45-minute interview with the Prince and Princess of Wales by the deferential broadcaster Alastair Burnett. Diana told him her most important role was 'supporting my husband whenever I can and always being behind him and also, most important, being a wife and mother'. Unfortunately, this wasn't what she was telling the Queen during their occasional meetings, when Diana poured out her heart to her mother-in-law. The monarch, either unwilling or unable to help, was reluctant to get involved. Counselling patience, she told the Princess: 'Just wait and see what happens.'

In an earlier bid to boost Diana's confidence, Her Majesty had issued a statement in April 1984 that said: 'The Queen could not be more pleased with her daughter-in-law. She is very proud of the Princess's activities around the world and at home.' Two years later, to her great dismay, the Queen was made aware that Prince Charles had resumed his relationship with Camilla Parker Bowles. Diana was also having affairs, beginning with Household Cavalry officer James Hewitt.

She also realised that Anne's marriage was in trouble. In April 1989 Scotland Yard launched a top-level investigation following the theft of four letters, said to be 'tender and affectionate', which were sent to the Princess Royal by the Queen's equerry, Commander Timothy Laurence. The affair prompted speculation that the Princess's 15-year marriage was falling apart. Finally, on 30 August, Buckingham Palace announced that Anne and Mark were to separate, though there were 'no plans to divorce'.

For the Queen, the 1980s ended on a sad note. To her former Private Secretary, Martin Charteris, she remarked: 'I thought I had brought them up so well.' Later she asked a lady-in-waiting poignantly: 'Where did we go wrong?'

Little did she realise that in the next decade things would get an awful lot worse.

142   The Queen's Diamond Jubilee

CHAPTER 7

The 1990s

by INGRID SEWARD

THE YEARS FROM 1990 to 1999 were the most exacting, difficult and draining of the Queen's reign. As soon as she had overcome one problem, another – more horrendous than before – replaced it. Nothing in her life had prepared the Queen for the troubles that overwhelmed her family in the years leading up to the *denouement* of her *annus horribilis* in 1992. In the past she had had to deal with bereavements, her sister's personal problems and her husband's alleged infidelities. She had sat in counsel with nine prime ministers and visited most of the world's countries. Over the span of half a century she had met nearly all the great leaders of the age – some good, many bad, a few utterly deranged – and handled them all with grace and finesse. In that time she had shown herself to be a woman of will determined to carry out her duties in her own way and according to her own beliefs. She had seen the influence of the monarchy eroded, but had steadfastly maintained her personal authority.

The 1990s changed everything. It saw the separation and subsequent divorce of three of her four children; the popularity of the institution she had devoted her life to wane; a fire devastate her beloved Windsor Castle; Buckingham Palace open to the public; her personal income taxed for the first time; and of course the media havoc wreaked by the popularity and eventual tragic death of Diana, Princess of Wales.

It all started with a financial overhaul, which included reforms on the way Buckingham Palace was run. Her Majesty's income and wealth were arousing great interest at the beginning of the 1990s, and one of Margaret Thatcher's last actions as Prime Minister was to put the Civil List on a sounder footing. The settlement was in the nick of time as public and political opinion, already strained by reports of the extravagance of the younger members of the royal family, was losing sympathy on the issue of money. The Queen was said by various publications to be the richest woman in the world and it was claimed that shrewd investments had raised her untaxed income by 20 per cent in one year alone.

The Queen's Diamond Jubilee 143

THE 1990s

The tabloids claimed the monarch saved more than £256 million on income tax, but as always the subject of royal finances was a confusing one. The Palace pointed out for the umpteenth time that the Queen owning something did not necessarily mean that she could sell it and pocket the cash.

To many taxpayers the distinction between disposable wealth and being a custodian of so much property hardly mattered, but because of the behaviour of the younger members of the royal family it was brought sharply into focus. Many decided the House of Windsor was 'an expensive luxury' and in 1991 the issue became more prominent, partly because of the short-lived Gulf War.

The media said the royal family should be setting a better example at a time of national emergency and objected to 'Viscount Linley in drag at a party', 'Fergie spending £5 million on a house that's always empty' and Prince Andrew playing golf on 'sunny Spanish links'.

It was the first criticism of the royal family in wartime for a decade and it was even predicted that the Queen would use her Christmas broadcast at the end of 1991 to declare her intention to abdicate in favour of her eldest son.

It never happened, of course, but because of the general sense of apathy surrounding the monarchy the Queen decided that the 40th anniversary of her accession, 6 February 1992, was to be suitably low-key. She discouraged any festivities and a plan to erect a fountain in Parliament Square was dropped at her request.

The milestone was marked, however, by the BBC documentary *Elizabeth R*, which showed a relatively informal 65-year-old monarch at work in her various homes, preparing speeches, making official visits and with her family at Balmoral Castle.

The year started badly and got increasingly worse. The Queen was confronted in January 1992 by her favourite son Prince Andrew and his wife telling her that their marriage was all but over. The meeting was brief and painful and

Sarah later wrote: 'She asked me to reconsider, to be strong and go forward'. To placate the Queen, the Yorks agreed to delay any final decision for six months. But this patchwork solution did not last, as later in January embarrassing photographs of the Duchess of York with her lover Steve Wyatt, an American playboy, were published, leading to a legal separation in March. Princess Anne's separation from Mark Phillips was formalised and the couple divorced in April.

In May, Sarah was seen to pack up and leave the marital home, Sunninghill, with her daughters Princesses Beatrice and Eugenie. And all the while the 'War of the Waleses' occupied many of the newspaper front pages. In the current climate, with the success of the Duke and Duchess of Cambridge's marriage and the general upsurge of the popularity of the royal family, it is hard to remember just how bad things were in the 1990s. There was no direct criticism of the Queen, but Charles and Diana's disintegrating relationship and the increasingly crazy antics of the Duchess of York eroded the brand of royalty.

When the Queen and the Duke of Edinburgh visited Australia in 1992 they received a lukewarm reception compared with earlier visits. Prince Philip, ever the keeper of family affairs, told Diana and Sarah (in the nicest possible terms to the former but rather more vehemently to the latter) that their behaviour was damaging the institution of the monarchy, which the Queen had striven her whole life to uphold.

THE 1990s

According to Robert Lacey, the author of *Royal: Her Majesty Queen Elizabeth II*, 'the turning point in the history of the modern monarchy occurred in a transport café in North Ruislip in the summer of 1991. Over bacon and eggs, Dr James Colhurst, a childhood friend of Diana, poured out to journalist Andrew Morton the Princess's catalogue of marital grievances and proposed that this should form the basis of a book, which Morton would write with the covert assistance of Diana, alongside the on-record testimony of her family and friends, whom she would authorise to speak.'

On 7 June 1992, when the book was first serialised in *The Sunday Times*, no detail of the agony that was the Waleses' marriage was spared. The Queen, still clinging to the delusion that the situation could be salvaged, authorised her Private Secretary Robert Fellowes (who also happened to be Diana's brother-in-law) to speak to the Princess, so the Palace could deny her complicity in the book.

Diana told him it was nothing to do with her, and Fellowes and the Queen believed her. But by midweek the truth was out, and Diana was proven to be an accomplice; Fellowes did the honourable thing and offered the Queen his resignation. She refused it on the grounds it was

146 The Queen's Diamond Jubilee

her daughter-in-law and not her Private Secretary who was guilty of misleading her.

In most families this would have sparked an explosive bout of rows and recriminations and most likely an immediate end to the marriage, but the royal family is governed by its own needs and even at this juncture the Queen had the vain hope that given time the situation could be resolved.

Trooping the Colour took place on the Saturday after the first *Sunday Times* instalment, and Diana had to stand beside her mother-in-law on the balcony of Buckingham Place looking as if absolutely nothing were amiss. The following week she was at Royal Ascot with the rest of the royal family but the tension was there for all to see. Prince Philip snubbed Diana in full view of everyone in the Royal Enclosure, but at least she was there. Fergie wasn't.

Sarah had been banished to social Siberia and made the cardinal error of embarrassing the Queen when she stood with her daughters and watched the royal procession go past in Windsor Great Park on the way to the races. To make matters worse, she made Prince Andrew join her the next day and repeat the performance as a show of 'solidarity'.

The Queen's Diamond Jubilee 147

THE 1990s

The Prince and Princess of Wales had already had a 'summit' meeting with the Queen and Prince Philip at which Charles's parents had tried in vain to explain how they understood the problems a marriage can go through.

When the question of a separation was raised, the Queen insisted – as she had done with Princess Margaret when her marriage was collapsing – that they make yet another attempt to resolve their differences. It was the monarch talking, not the mother, but it only made the situation even more unpalatable.

Instinct suggested that the Waleses had long passed the point of reconciliation and should be allowed to go their separate ways. Yet even at such a late stage, this remained in the realms of the unthinkable for a sovereign whose throne rested on the foundation of a dutiful and – above all united – family. Unwilling to face up to the constitutional implications of a separation, the Queen instead ordered her favourite solution to Charles and Diana: a six-month cooling-off period.

If July provided a respite, August brought the Queen a double dose of trouble. Balmoral is Her Majesty's holiday home and although the court is officially in Scotland and she works on her state boxes every day, the tranquillity of the Highlands allows the Queen some time to herself. She loves it. Nothing is allowed to disturb the peace of her Scottish break, but quite often something does.

In this case it was photographs of a topless Duchess of York sunbathing beside a pool in the south of France with her 'financial advisor' John Bryan kneeling at her feet sucking her toes. The unfortunate Fergie, although separated from Prince Andrew, was staying at Balmoral with her daughters when the story broke in the *Daily Mirror*.

The Queen, Sarah recalled, was 'furious'. She did not scream or shout; that is not her way. Rather she was cold and abrupt as she berated her daughter-in-law for exposing the monarchy to such ridicule.

'Her anger wounded me to the core,' Fergie said later, but for the sake of the children she was forced to spend three more humiliating days at Balmoral before returning to her rented home at Wentworth.

148 The Queen's Diamond Jubilee

But by the week's end it was Diana's turn to come under the lash – with far greater consequence to the royal family. In response to the *Daily Mirror*'s scoop *The Sun* decided the time was right to publish the transcript of a three-year-old telephone conversation between the Princess and her friend James Gilbey. He called her 'Squidgy' constantly during the 23-minute recording, which contained Diana's disparaging observations about the royal family and her husband.

In a tearful conversation Diana tried to persuade the Queen that she was being set up and hinted darkly that she believed some of her mother-in-law's courtiers were conspiring to discredit her. The Queen dismissed this for the nonsense it was – her much-tried patience with Diana was running out, but she still clung to the hope that things might change and the marriage be salvaged. Like his mother, Prince Charles clung forlornly to the hope that the marriage could somehow be saved and plans went ahead for the couple's scheduled trip to Korea in the autumn. It was, as predicted, a disaster, as there for all to see was a couple who could clearly no longer stand the sight of each other. This was compounded when in November the transcript of yet another illicit recording, the 'Camillagate' tape, was published. In this, the most sensational recorded conversation so far, the Prince of Wales spoke to his mistress touchingly and absurdly and with reckless indiscretion.

THE 1990s

150 The Queen's Diamond Jubilee

CHAPTER 7

If the Queen's subjects imagined that the royal family discussed these scandals openly they were mistaken. That is not the royal way, although perhaps it should be. Although things were not comfortable at Balmoral that summer, Princess Margaret assured a friend that the Queen kept off the topic and the guests did not raise it.

The Queen's children have described how difficult it was to get their mother to discuss anything unpalatable. Like the Queen Mother, she has always compartmentalised things and avoided moral confrontation. Had she been a different character she might have tackled the problem of Charles and Diana far earlier and found a solution, but she was – and still is – wary of interfering in her children's private affairs.

She was as surprised as anyone, for instance, when in 1989 Princess Anne announced she was separating from Mark Phillips. In April 1992 they were divorced and by the following December Anne had married the Queen's former equerry, Tim Laurence, then a commander in the Royal Navy.

Although the Queen preferred to take a back seat as far as the private lives of her children were concerned, she was thrust into the drama between Charles and Diana. It was yet another row over their sons, who should have brought them together, which finally brought down the curtain on the Waleses' marriage. Back from Korea, Charles arranged a shooting weekend at Sandringham to coincide with William and Harry's *exeat* from Ludgrove, their prep school. Diana refused to go and informed Charles she was taking the boys to Windsor instead.

Charles snapped and telephoned the Queen. When she again pleaded patience, he abandoned the training of a lifetime and shouted down the line at his mother. 'Don't you realise? She's mad, mad, mad!' And with that he slammed the receiver down.

The royal family was going up in smoke – literally – as on 20 November 1992 Windsor Castle was engulfed by flames. The fire was started by a restorer's lamp, which set a curtain alight. It quickly spread through the private chapel and devoured St George's Hall. Prince Andrew organised the rescue of many treasures, but great parts of the building itself were consumed by the blaze. A corner of Windsor Castle, the symbol of the monarchy for almost a thousand years, had nearly been reduced to smouldering rubble. It was the Queen and the Duke of Edinburgh's 45th wedding anniversary but Philip was overseas at the time.

The Queen's Diamond Jubilee

THE 1990s

Two days later the Queen was at Guildhall in the City of London for a luncheon to mark the 40th anniversary of her accession. The Prime Minister, John Major, had just announced she was going to pay tax on her private income, telling the House of Commons that the initiative had come from the monarch herself, the decision having been made the previous summer. The timing was not good, but then nothing was that year, as the Queen expressed herself. With Philip back at her side, she said in a voice hoarse with flu and emotion: '1992 is not a year on which I shall look back with undiluted pleasure. In the words of one of my more sympathetic correspondents, it has turned out to be an *annus horribilis*.'

There was even worse to come, as the Queen already knew. On 9 December 1992 the Prime Minister stood up in the House of Commons and made a statement. 'It is announced from Buckingham Palace that, with regret, the Prince and Princess of Wales have decided to separate,' he said. 'The decision has been reached amicably, and they will continue to participate fully in the upbringing of their children… The Queen and the Duke of Edinburgh, though saddened, understand and sympathise with the difficulties which have led to this decision…'

The Queen was at Wood Farm on the Sandringham estate with only a handful of staff when the announcement was made. She did not watch the Prime Minister on television. Instead she did what she always did when agitated: she took her corgis for a walk through the wintery woods and ploughed fields of her Norfolk estate.

When she returned a member of her staff said how sorry he was to hear the news. 'I think you'll find it's all for the best,' the Queen replied.

152 The Queen's Diamond Jubilee

CHAPTER 7

The Queen's Diamond Jubilee 153

THE 1990s

If the Queen was exhausted by the events of 1992, the next few years provided little respite from what the press dubbed 'The War of the Waleses'. In the autumn of 1994, an authorised biography written by journalist and broadcaster Jonathan Dimbleby appeared to mark the 25th anniversary of Charles's investiture as Prince of Wales. Its publication was preceded by a lengthy BBC interview with the Prince.

The book aroused interest as it gave a full account of Charles's relationship with Camilla Parker Bowles, but more upsetting for the Queen were the details, albeit brief, of how Charles saw his relationship with his parents. The Queen was presented as cold; Prince Philip as a bully. To compound matters the book was serialised in *The Sunday Times* at the same time as Her Majesty's historic state visit to Russia.

The Queen was so concerned at the effect that Diana and Charles's media shenanigans were having on the institution of the monarchy that she managed to convince herself that no one would turn up at Buckingham Palace in May 1995 for the 50th anniversary of VE-Day, the end of the Second World War in Europe. Throughout the early morning she kept looking out of the window, anxiously checking to see if anyone was there. But by the time she made her balcony appearance with the 94-year-old Queen Mother and Princess Margaret, the area in front of Buckingham Palace was packed with people.

'Her Majesty was thrilled,' a member of her staff revealed later. 'When she went on to the balcony she remained stony-faced for fear of showing too much emotion. She was actually close to tears.'

The commemorations seemed to revive the bond between monarchy and people.

The sight of three elderly women, in contrasting colours, standing together as they had stood five decades earlier, was deeply affecting and the Queen was touched and reassured by the public response. Her happiness was, however, once again to be short lived.

Despite her misgivings and aggravation with her daughter-in-law, the Queen had continued to be accommodating with Diana. While Prince Philip raged, the Queen stuck to her guns and continued to insist that the Princess needed support, not condemnation. She knew Diana's glamour and hands-on charity work had won her global approval, but subsequent events proved too much for even the Queen.

Diana had been outraged by her husband's Dimbleby interview, which she saw as a riposte to the Morton book and, as such, a deliberate attempt to discredit her. In fact, Charles had been very careful not to voice any criticism of his wife. The accompanying biography, however, made it quite clear that many of the Prince's coterie regarded her as mentally unstable. It was a charge she was determined to refute and to do that she too chose the medium of television.

In an hour-long interview broadcast on BBC *Panorama* on 20 November 1995, watched by the largest British television audience ever, at that time, she admitted adultery with James Hewitt, indicated she did not expect Charles to be King, and offered her elder son as an alternative. And she said she would like to be 'Queen of People's Hearts'.

THE 1990s

156 The Queen's Diamond Jubilee

CHAPTER 7

On the night of the broadcast the Queen attended the Royal Variety Performance; it was her 48th wedding anniversary. In the days after the interview, which she was blissfully unaware of until an hour and a half before the broadcast when the BBC announced their scoop, the Queen consulted the Prime Minister, the Archbishop of Canterbury and senior royal staff. Then in early December she made a pre-emptive strike – writing letters to both the Prince and Princess giving it as her own opinion, with her husband's support, that an early divorce was desirable.

On 28 August 1996, Charles and Diana were divorced. The fairytale that had become a gothic nightmare was almost at its end. Diana, Princess of Wales, as she was now to be known, had one year and three days left to live.

The Queen, who had celebrated her 70th birthday that April, carried on as before. She might have led a more solitary existence than in the past as a number of her friends had 'gone to greener pastures', as the Queen Mother was fond of saying. Patrick Plunket had died in 1975; Rupert Neville in 1982. Her mother, one of the pillars of her life, had a successful hip operation in 1995 and seemed immortal. However, in September 1993, Margaret 'Bobo' MacDonald – nursemaid at 145 Piccadilly and then royal dresser, companion, confidante and friend for 67 years – died at the age of 89. When Prince Philip was away the Queen frequently dined alone, but the continuing domestic crises brought her closer to Princess Anne and the two women were often seen walking together in the palace garden deep in conversation. For the first time the Queen listened to someone other than her husband on family matters and valued her daughter's forthright opinions.

In March 1996 they travelled to Dunblane together to visit the families of 16 schoolchildren and their teacher who had been shot in a massacre. The Scottish press recorded the Queen weeping openly and turning to Princess Anne for support as she spoke to the parents of the victims. A few days later it was business as usual when the Queen and the Duke of Edinburgh paid successful state visits to Poland and the Czech Republic.

The Queen's Diamond Jubilee 157

THE 1990s

At the beginning of August 1997 the Queen boarded the soon-to-be decommissioned Royal Yacht *Britannia* for the last of the Western Isles cruises. With 16 members of her family on board, she was looking forward to the cruise followed by a peaceful two months in Scotland.

The court was thus at Balmoral when the Queen's acting Private Secretary, Robin Janvrin, received a call from the British Embassy in Paris to say that Diana, Princess of Wales had been involved in a car crash. He looked at his watch and saw it was shortly before 1am on Sunday 31 August. The severity of the accident was unclear at first, but Janvrin immediately informed the Queen and Prince Charles, who was also at Balmoral at the time with his sons. The Prince resolved to travel to France to be at her side, but as a flight was being arranged Janvrin took another call, this time informing him that the Princess was dead. It was 4am.

Upset though she was (her first reaction had been that someone had 'greased the brakes' to get rid of the Princess), the Queen decided it should be business as usual and the whole family would go to church at nearby Crathie that morning. William and Harry, who had been told of the tragedy by their father, agreed to go too.

The funeral, the Queen is alleged to have said, should be a family affair at Windsor followed by interment in the royal burial ground at Frogmore; Robert Fellowes is said to have agreed. The situation was, however, being wrested from her control as the crowds of mourners who gathered in London as the days progressed were perilously close to turning into a mob. Repeating tabloid sentiments, they demanded to know why no flag was flying at half mast from Buckingham Palace, why no royal tributes to the Princess had been forthcoming and above all else why the royal family had chosen to remain in Scotland instead of returning to the capital to join the nation's mourning.

The Queen returned to London on the eve of Diana's funeral. She was driven straight to Buckingham Palace where, with Prince Philip at her side, she left the safety of her car and went to mingle with the heaving throng gathered outside the flower-covered railings.

Dressed in black, she walked down the line of mourners in total silence until an 11-year-old girl handed her some roses. 'Would you like me to place them for you? asked the Queen. 'No, Your Majesty,' the girl replied. 'They are for you.'

'The crowd began to applaud,' an aide recalled. 'I remember thinking "Gosh; it's all right".'

CHAPTER 7

The Queen's Diamond Jubilee 159

THE 1990s

The Queen was more her usual self by the time she made a live television broadcast that evening. With the composure that comes from a lifetime's training, she addressed the nation 'as your Queen and as a grandmother', paying tribute to Diana, explaining the royal family's decision to stay in Scotland and promising a new beginning.

'I for one,' she said, 'believe there are lessons to be drawn from her life and from the extraordinary and moving reaction to her death.'

The funeral proved difficult for the Queen, as not only was she genuinely upset but also she was obliged to sit opposite her godson Earl Spencer in Westminster Abbey while he articulated his extraordinary address with its veiled threats. He said he would do everything he could to make sure William and Harry's souls were 'not simply immersed by duty and tradition, but can sing openly as you [Diana] planned'.

The year ended on a far happier note when the Queen and Prince Philip celebrated their Golden Wedding anniversary. Besides a service of thanksgiving at Westminster Abbey and other public celebrations, the Queen gave a dinner dance at the newly restored Windsor Castle. Despite the grandeur of the setting, it was said to be the most relaxed and informal gathering of European royalty that anyone can remember, which was exactly what the Queen had hoped for. In her Christmas broadcast she described the tragic events of August 1997 as 'almost unbearably sad' and said 'we all felt the shock and sorrow of Diana's death'.

Towards the end of 1998 the Queen faced an unprecedented outburst during her speech at the State Opening of Parliament. As the monarch outlined her government's plan to ban most hereditary peers from sitting in the House of Lords she was interrupted by shouts of 'hear hear' from Labour MPs. It was a considerable act of discourtesy and the first time in living memory that the sovereign's address had been interrupted. The speech is the pinnacle of the unique constitutional relationship that exists between Crown and Parliament and is traditionally heard in silence, as a mark of respect if nothing else. The royal family have made it clear they no longer expect people to bow or curtsey to them unless they want to do so, but interruptions are strictly taboo.

The increasingly informality of her Labour government occupied Her Majesty's thoughts again at the end of 1999 when she was obliged to hold hands with Prime Minister Tony Blair (rather than the traditional linking of arms) and sing *Auld Lang Syne* at the Millennium Dome, which she had officially opened just before midnight.

There was some happiness to end the distressing decade of the 1990s, however, when the Queen's youngest son Prince Edward married his long-term girlfriend Sophie Rhys-Jones at St George's Chapel, Windsor Castle. There were no grand processions: the late-afternoon ceremony was followed by a carriage drive through Windsor by the newlyweds and a reception in the state apartments. It was low key for a royal wedding but considered fitting for the times, just as Prince William's marriage to Catherine Middleton in Westminster Abbey was 12 years later.

CHAPTER 7

The Queen's Diamond Jubilee 161

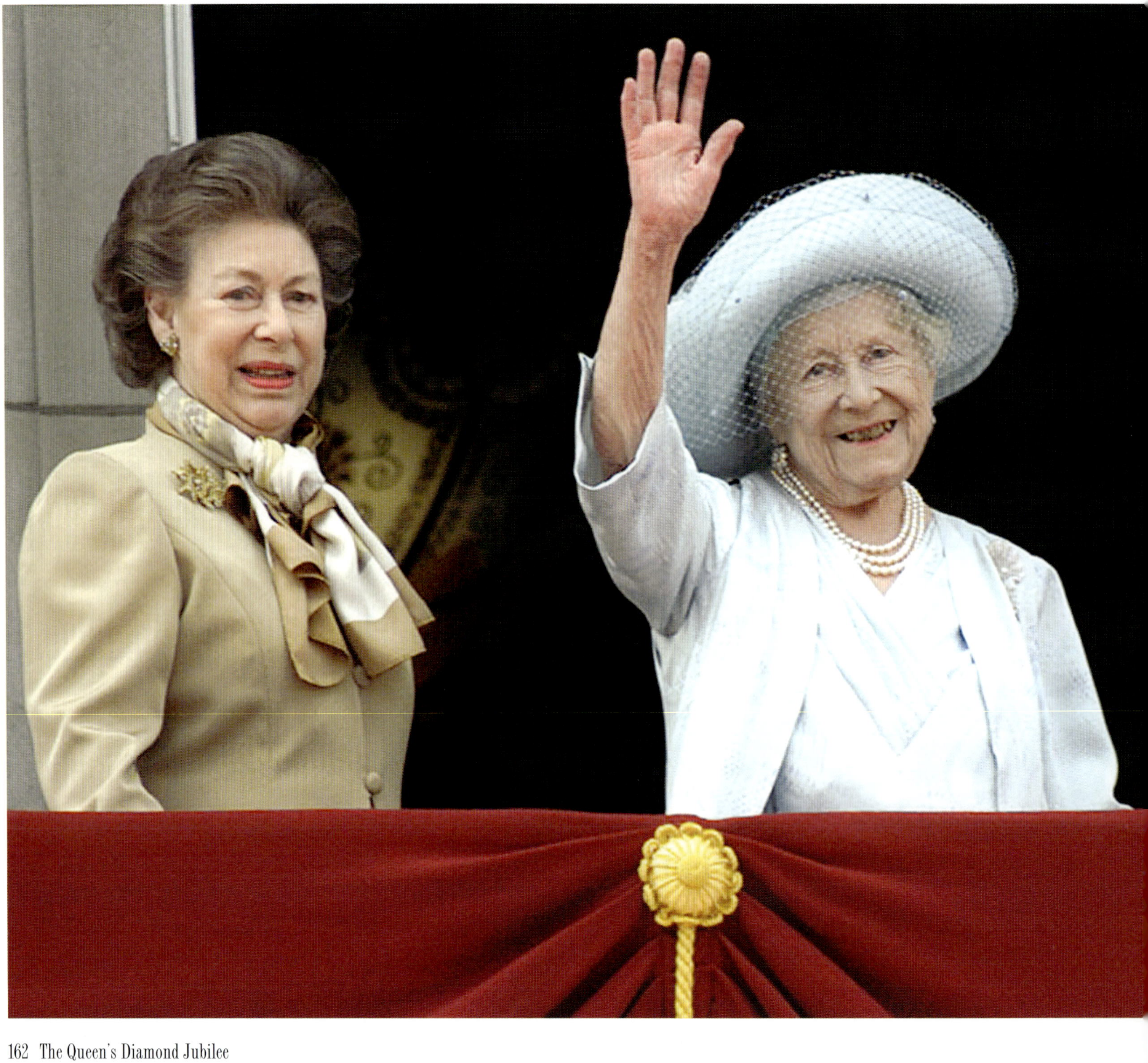

CHAPTER 8

The 2000s

by CORYNE HALL

AS THE NEW millennium dawned the Queen was approaching her 74th birthday but, despite reaching an age when most people were enjoying retirement, she showed no signs of letting up. During the first decade of the 21st century she carried out a full programme of engagements and undertook 28 official overseas tours, starting with a visit to Australia in March.

Coming just four months after the referendum in which, by a narrow majority, Australia voted to keep the Queen as head of state, the monarch was well aware that the situation was delicate. In an historic speech at Sydney Opera House, she said that Australia's constitutional future was entirely a matter for the people. 'Whatever the future may bring,' she added, 'my lasting respect and deep affection for Australia and Australians everywhere will remain as strong as ever.' The two-week tour was a triumph.

Back home the Queen gave a ball at Windsor Castle to celebrate four milestone birthdays: Prince Andrew's 40th, Princess Anne's 50th, Princess Margaret's 70th and the Queen Mother's 100th. On 4 August 2000 she derived great pleasure in sending her mother a handwritten congratulatory message, which Queen Elizabeth opened ceremoniously outside Clarence House – with the help of her equerry and his sword – to the delight of onlookers.

The following year, Prince Philip's 80th birthday, a more low-key affair, was celebrated with a service of thanksgiving and a reception at Windsor Castle.

The Queen's Diamond Jubilee 163

THE 2000s

Politically, the decade was dominated by a Labour government after Tony Blair led the party to victory for a second term in the 2001 General Election. Shortly afterwards, on 11 September, the terrorist group Al-Qaeda launched suicide attacks on New York's World Trade Center, the Pentagon in Washington and in Pennsylvania too, in which some 3,000 people were killed. As a sign of solidarity the Queen allowed *The Star-Spangled Banner* to be played during the changing of the guard at Buckingham Palace a few days later. In response to the attacks, British and American forces moved into Afghanistan.

The Golden Jubilee year, 2002, started badly with the death of Princess Margaret on 9 February after a long illness. The Queen's grief was heightened by worry over her mother's frail health; to lighten the blow, the 101-year-old Queen Mother was initially told that the Princess was desperately ill in hospital. Later the Queen gently broke the news that she had died.

Despite her loss, shortly after her sister's funeral the Queen travelled to Kingston, Jamaica, for the first stage of a planned tour. The Jamaicans (who fondly call her 'Missis Queen') lifted her spirits and the Queen carried out her duties with customary aplomb, although not without a hitch.

One evening the electricity supply failed as she was dressing for dinner. Making her way carefully downstairs by the light of a kerosene lamp, the Queen momentarily lost her cool as she and Prince Philip were blinded by photographers' flashlights.

'No flash; no photographs. I can't see,' she said somewhat testily.

The royal couple moved on to New Zealand and Australia and after circumnavigating the globe returned home to find Queen Elizabeth the Queen Mother was failing visibly. She died peacefully on 30 March, seven weeks after Princess Margaret, with her elder daughter at her bedside.

People queued for hours for the lying-in-state in Westminster Hall, the line snaking over Lambeth Bridge and away into the distance. On the evening before the Queen Mother's funeral, the Queen made a televised broadcast to thank the public for their tributes to her mother, adding that she had 'drawn great comfort from so many individual acts of kindness and respect'.

Despite this bitter double blow, between February and October she and Prince Philip visited 70 cities and towns in the United Kingdom as part of their Golden Jubilee tour. At 10 Downing Street in April the Queen was present for an historic dinner with the five surviving Prime Ministers who had served during her reign.

The Golden Jubilee weekend began with the first of two public concerts held in the garden of Buckingham Palace. Some 200 million people worldwide watched the concerts on live television, and subsequently sales of the CDs earned the Queen the first gold disc awarded to a member of the royal family. On 4 June, the Gold State Coach took the Queen and Prince Philip in a ceremonial procession to St Paul's Cathedral for a service of thanksgiving. That afternoon, after a lunch hosted by the Lord Mayor of London at Guildhall, formality gave way to fun as a cavalcade of floats marking 50 glorious years swept down The Mall to Buckingham Palace. When the Queen appeared on the balcony she seemed surprised and delighted by the warmth of the public's affection; her special day ended with a flypast by Concorde and the Red Arrows display team.

Later that month many of Europe's reigning sovereigns and their consorts converged on Windsor Castle for the annual Order of the Garter service. A formal dinner was held in the Waterloo Chamber that evening and the following day some of them were present at Royal Ascot, making the traditional drive down the racecourse a truly royal occasion.

THE 2000s

166 The Queen's Diamond Jubilee

CHAPTER 8

The momentous year ended with the dramatic acquittal of Paul Burrell, former butler to Diana, Princess of Wales, who had been charged with stealing items from her estate. Nine days into the Old Bailey trial, the Queen told Prince Philip and Prince Charles that she recalled Burrell saying that he was looking after some of the Princess's possessions. The trial was halted.

Meanwhile, the inquest into the death of Diana and her companion Dodi Fayed dragged on and on. Only in April 2008 did a jury decide by a majority verdict that the couple had been unlawfully killed by a combination of the driving of their Mercedes by their chauffeur Henri Paul, who was alleged to be drunk, and the pursuing paparazzi photographers.

In early 2003 a multinational force led by the US and Britain invaded Iraq to topple the regime of Saddam Hussein, who they believed was harbouring weapons of mass destruction.

The war proved controversial, and when President George W. Bush visited London that November there were protests in Trafalgar Square. Security was tight, but the Queen was not amused when, only hours before the President's arrival at Buckingham Palace, it was revealed that an undercover tabloid reporter had been working there as a footman having used false references.

Coming as it did just months after the 'comedian' Aaron Barschak gatecrashed Prince William's 21st birthday party at Windsor Castle, it highlighted serious flaws in royal security.

The Iraq war had strained Franco-British relations and thus the Queen's 2004 visit to France to celebrate the centenary of the signing of the *Entente Cordiale* required delicate handling. She travelled by train through the Channel Tunnel to Paris and, despite security fears after the recent Madrid terrorist bombings, surprised her hosts by going on several walkabouts.

Cheers and shouts of '*Vive la Reine*' could soon be heard. The Queen urged France and Britain to bury their short-term differences and work towards a more unified Europe, although not at the expense of America.

In November the Queen and the Duke of Edinburgh visited Berlin. German newspapers had suggested she should apologise for the wartime bombing of Dresden, which killed 35,000 people, but she did not do so. Instead the Queen emphasised the appalling suffering of war 'and how precious is the peace we have built in Europe since 1945'.

The Queen's Diamond Jubilee 167

THE 2000s

There were also 'firsts'. In October 2006 the Queen visited the Baltic states of Lithuania, Latvia and Estonia, which became independent from the former Soviet Union in 1991. She was greeted enthusiastically, so much so that before one lunch in Latvia they played three verses of the National Anthem instead of just the usual one. Prince Philip, caught unawares, had started to sit down when the music struck up again. As the third verse finished he was heard to mutter, 'Is that all?'

Ten years after the Good Friday Agreement, Northern Ireland was the destination in March 2008. During the historic three-day visit the traditional Royal Maundy service was held in the 12th-century St Patrick's Church of Ireland Cathedral in Armagh, the first time the ceremony had been held outside England or Wales. Although security was tight, the Queen carried out a number of engagements and there were only a few minor demonstrations.

Even more sensitive was her state visit to Turkey that May, to bolster Britain's support for the country's bid to join the European Union despite strong French and German opposition. Further controversy was caused when the devout Muslim wife of Turkey's new Islamist President, Abdullah Gül, defied Turkish law and wore a religious headscarf to greet the monarch.

In 2008 there was an incoming state visit by French President Nicolas Sarkozy and his wife Carla Bruni, whose beauty and elegance turned all heads. Madame Bruni-Sarkozy was surprised to be conducted to her suite by the Queen personally, she later revealed.

By now, in a rare concession to age, evening engagements seldom appeared in the Queen's diary. Although she normally enjoyed robust health, in January 2003 she underwent surgery on her right knee after wrenching it while out walking. She left London's King Edward VII Hospital the following day walking with the aid of a stick. In December she returned to the hospital for keyhole surgery to remove torn cartilage from her other knee.

One of the more contentious family issues was the relationship of the Prince of Wales and Mrs Camilla Parker Bowles. The Queen was anxious that it be regularised long before he became King; after consultation with the Prime Minister, in 2005 she formally gave her son permission to marry. It was announced that a civil ceremony would take place at Windsor Castle on 8 April, followed by a service of prayer and dedication in St George's Chapel.

CHAPTER 8

It was far from plain sailing. First it was discovered that if Windsor Castle were licensed for weddings then other couples would have to be allowed to marry there, so Windsor Guildhall was substituted. Then the ceremony had to be postponed to allow Prince Charles to attend the funeral at the Vatican of Pope John Paul II who, as a head of state, required the presence of a high-profile representative.

When the couple married on 9 April neither the Queen nor Prince Philip attended the civil ceremony, preferring to attend the religious service instead. Afterwards, in an allusion to racing, the Queen warmly welcomed the bride and bridegroom into the 'winner's enclosure'. At her own request Camilla took the title Duchess of Cornwall rather than Princess of Wales. The Queen later changed the female order of precedence so that, when not accompanying her husband, Camilla ranked below Princess Anne and Princess Alexandra, both princesses by birth.

The Queen's Diamond Jubilee 169

THE 2000s

170 The Queen's Diamond Jubilee

CHAPTER 8

The decade gave the Queen two more grandchildren and witnessed the marriage of her first, Peter Phillips. The first child of the Earl and Countess of Wessex was born prematurely on 8 November 2002. Sophie Wessex had been rushed to the local NHS hospital at Frimley, Surrey, suffering from severe internal pains and blood loss. Delivered by emergency Caesarean, little Louise Alice Elizabeth Mary had to spend two weeks apart from her mother in intensive care in a London hospital. The Queen, who is very fond of Sophie, was deeply concerned and was later said to dote on her youngest granddaughter.

On 17 December 2007 Sophie gave birth to James Alexander Philip Theo, giving the delighted Queen and Duke their eighth grandchild. In accordance with Edward and Sophie's wish that their children would not be princes or princesses, they have been given the courtesy titles of the children of an earl. James is Viscount Severn, while his sister is Lady Louise Mountbatten-Windsor.

On 5 May 2005 Tony Blair's Labour government was elected for a third term, although with a reduced majority. Shortly afterwards there was an outcry when the government announced that the Queen would not be invited to commemorations for the 60th anniversary of VE-Day. Critics saw it as a snub to the monarch who, instead, attended events marking the 60th anniversary of the liberation of the Channel Islands.

However, a combined 60th anniversary of VE- and VJ-Day was marked in London on 10 July 2005, three days after the suicide bombings on the capital's transport system that killed 56 people and injured 700 others. The Queen used her speech to reflect that during the present difficulties people turned to the example 'of resilience, humour, sustained courage, often under conditions of great deprivation' shown by the wartime generation.

The Queen celebrated her 80th birthday on 21 April 2006. Some 40,000 congratulatory messages arrived from the public and on the day a massive crowd turned out to greet the monarch, who emerged from the Henry VIII Gate of Windsor Castle for a walkabout to the strains of *Happy Birthday* played by the Irish Guards. For 45 minutes the Queen accepted flowers, cards, poems and gifts galore with a beaming smile. At a candlelit family dinner in the newly restored Kew Palace that evening, the Prince of Wales paid a moving tribute to his mother's 'lifetime of service and dedication to her country, to her family, to the realms and the countries of the Commonwealth'.

The Queen's Diamond Jubilee 171

THE 2000s

In June the Queen's Birthday Parade was followed by the first ever *feu de joie* (fire of joy), three short blasts of blank shot fired in the air by 80 guardsmen lined up on the Palace forecourt. The public celebrations continued with a party for 2,000 children in the garden at Buckingham Palace, the highlight of which was a live television play, *The Queen's Handbag*, revolving around the theft of Her Majesty's most famous accessory containing the spectacles she would need to read her speech. The Queen gamely played along, coming on stage to retrieve the newly found handbag and wave her spectacles in the air. 'I do like happy endings!' she said gamely.

Since the decommissioning of the Royal Yacht *Britannia* in 1997 the Queen had missed her annual cruise around Scotland, so in her 80th year she decided on a treat. In July she chartered the MV *Hebridean Princess* (at a reported cost of £125,000) for an eight-day voyage around the Western Isles. The Queen was in high spirits as she greeted well-wishers on the quay at Port Ellen on Islay. The itinerary was not announced for security reasons, so

172 The Queen's Diamond Jubilee

CHAPTER 8

consequently the newsagent on the tiny island of Gigha was astounded when the Princess Royal walked in and asked if there was a taxi that could take the Queen to the famous Achamore Gardens. Explaining that there were no taxis, he cheerfully drove the monarch there himself. The cruise ended in Stornoway on the Isle of Lewis, where 200 people watched the royal family disembark.

The Queen continues to keep abreast of changes in technology. In 2001 Prince Andrew gave her a mobile telephone with the family's numbers programmed in, so that she could contact them on speed dial. The Duke of York has apparently also given her a BlackBerry, which allows access to email wherever she happens to be, although she is said to dictate her messages rather than write them herself. Prince William gave her an iPod and is believed to have shown her how to store the *Last Night of the Proms* on it. However, the notoriously frugal Queen reportedly declared her new high-definition flatscreen television 'a waste of money'.

The Queen's Diamond Jubilee

THE 2000s

Although the monarch admitted in March 2005 that she had yet to use a computer, the Royal Channel on YouTube was launched two years later after Princesses Beatrice and Eugenie had persuaded their grandmother to do so. Soon afterwards a YouTube spokesman confirmed that in an unofficial race against the White House the Queen had scored more hits than President Bush's channel.

In 2007 her Christmas message was shown live on YouTube for the first time, and in 2009 the Queen clicked a remote control to launch the revamped monarchy website. That year it also became possible to follow the Queen and the royal family on Facebook and Twitter.

The 'special' relationship between Britain and America had come under strain over the Iraq war, so in May 2007 the Queen and Duke visited the United States to mark the 400th anniversary of the foundation of Jamestown, the first permanent English settlement.

In preparation for the visit the monarch granted the famed American photographer Annie Liebovitz a sitting at Buckingham Palace. The shoot was filmed for a documentary about a year in the Queen's life but caused huge controversy when a BBC preview showed the monarch apparently storming out during the session, when in fact she had been walking in. The BBC apologised for splicing the footage together out of sequence.

During his welcoming speech on the White House lawn, President Bush muddled his dates. 'You visited us for our bicentennial in seventeen seventy...' he began, before hastily correcting himself, 'er, 1976', amid gales of laughter.

The following evening the Queen evened the score when, hosting a dinner at the British Ambassador's residence, she began her speech, 'When I was last here in 1776...' to much hilarity.

The Queen took the United States by storm. During a weekend off she also fulfilled a lifetime's ambition by watching the Kentucky Derby, America's most famous horse race.

174 The Queen's Diamond Jubilee

As Head of the Armed Forces, it gave the Queen special pleasure to be present at two Sovereign's Parades at Sandhurst in 2006 when her grandsons passed out. In April it was the turn of Prince Harry, followed by William in December. Both began their Army service as officers in the Household Cavalry's Blues and Royals. As the war in Afghanistan dragged on, Harry naturally wished to join his men serving there but security issues made this difficult. The Queen supported him and at the end of 2007 was able to tell Harry that his wish would be granted.

A media blackout was enforced to prevent Harry, and those around him, becoming an enemy target, but the following February the disappointed Prince was recalled after details of his whereabouts were leaked on the internet.

The Queen spoke of her admiration, saying her grandson had performed 'a good job in a very difficult climate'. In 2009, as the casualty lists grew longer, the Queen gave her name to the Elizabeth Cross, designed to honour the families of Armed Forces personnel killed in battle or by terrorism since 1945.

Tony Blair decided to step down as Prime Minister and submitted his resignation to the Queen in June 2007. Her Majesty was advised to ask Gordon Brown, who had become the unopposed leader of the Labour Party a few days earlier, to form a government. He was the 11th Prime Minister of her reign.

On 20 November 2007 the Queen became the first monarch to celebrate a Diamond Wedding anniversary. Her children, six eldest grandchildren and four remaining bridesmaids were among the congregation for a thanksgiving service at Westminster Abbey a day earlier. The Queen decided that a party was inappropriate at a time when the UK was going into recession.

Instead, *en route* to Uganda, she and Prince Philip stopped off in Malta to relive some of the memories of early married life. Before leaving London the Queen presented her husband with the Royal Victorian Chain, an honour in her own gift, as a sign of her 'esteem and affection'.

THE 2000s

On 22 December of that year, the Queen, at the age of 81 years, seven months, four weeks and two days, surpassed her great-great-grandmother Queen Victoria as the oldest-serving monarch. The Duke of Edinburgh notched up his own record in April 2009, when he became the longest-serving consort of a reigning monarch.

Another landmark was reached on 5 March 2008 when the Queen overtook the Plantagenet King Henry III to become the country's third-longest-reigning sovereign, after George III (59 years, 96 days) and Queen Victoria, who reigned for almost 64 years. That June Her Majesty proudly invested Prince William as a Royal Knight Companion of the Order of the Garter, the 1,000th Knight in the register.

Peter Phillips became the first of the Queen's grandchildren to marry when, on 17 May 2008, he wed Canadian-born Autumn Kelly at St George's Chapel. The Queen was said to have been less than amused when the couple sold the photographs in an exclusive deal with a celebrity magazine.

As 2009 dawned, the Queen and the Duke cancelled a state visit to the Gulf States. It was the first time within memory that such a visit had been cancelled except for war or terrorism. Buckingham Palace denied rumours of ill health, blaming a diary clash. The visit went ahead in November 2010.

176 The Queen's Diamond Jubilee

CHAPTER 8

The Queen's Diamond Jubilee 177

THE 2000s

In April the new American President Barack Obama attended the G20 summit in London, before which he and his wife Michelle had a private meeting with the Queen and the Duke. Her Majesty and Mrs Obama struck up a mutual rapport and were seen to put their arms around each other as they talked. Later the monarch placed her hand on Mrs Obama's back in a spontaneous gesture of affection. They kept in touch and a few weeks later Mrs Obama was back in London with her daughters for tea with the Queen and a private tour of Buckingham Palace.

After the royal finances had come under scrutiny in 2002 Buckingham Palace began disclosing exactly how the Queen spends taxpayers' money. In June 2009 the Queen sought the first increase in the Civil List for nearly 20 years in order to plug a deficit of some five million pounds a year for the Royal Household. The Queen had been funding the deficit out of reserve cash and money was urgently needed for essential maintenance to the palaces. With the country undergoing an economic crisis and the news dominated by widespread outrage over MPs' alleged misuse of parliamentary expenses, it was not good timing and there were calls for her to open Buckingham Palace more frequently to raise money. The Queen had already expressed concern about the country's economy, asking, during a visit to the London School of Economics, why nobody had seen the credit crunch coming. In March 2009 she summoned Mervyn King, Governor of the Bank of England, for urgent talks.

Following increasing paparazzi intrusion into activities on the monarch's private estates the Queen warned newspapers that legal action would be taken if they published photographs of the royal family in 'private' situations. The move was thought to be designed to make the position clear, so that if Prince William eventually announced his engagement to Kate Middleton she would be protected from the harassment suffered by the late Princess of Wales.

In November 2009 the Queen was welcomed in Bermuda, almost 56 years to the day after her first visit. After marking the 400th anniversary of Britain's oldest colony she travelled to Trinidad and Tobago to open the 20th Commonwealth Heads of Government Meeting. On the eve of the meeting Gordon Brown was accused of using the occasion to seek the views of other Commonwealth nations regarding moves to change the law of succession to end male primogeniture and abolish the 1701 Act of Settlement, which bars Roman Catholics from the throne. The Palace was cautious about such changes, which would need the approval of all 16 countries of which the Queen is head of state.

The meeting marked the modern Commonwealth's 60th anniversary. Despite Zimbabwe's suspension in 2002 (and withdrawal in 2003) following the Mugabe regime's continued violence against white Rhodesian farmers, the monarch reflected on 'how far the Commonwealth has come in its 60 years, and yet how true it has remained to its origins'.

During her reign thus far the Queen has attended every one of CHOGM's meetings, even if only for the opening ceremony. Although the Queen's pace had slowed, as the decade closed the 83-year-old monarch showed no sign of wishing to take things easy.

180 The Queen's Diamond Jubilee

CHAPTER 9

The Present Day

by CHRISTOPHER WARWICK

THE START OF the second decade of the 21st century brought with it several significant events in the Queen's life, both of a political as well as a personal nature. Following the UK general election in May 2010, which saw an end to 13 years of New Labour but resulted in a hung parliament, giving no overall majority to any of the main parties, Her Majesty asked David Cameron, leader of the Conservatives, who had secured the largest vote, to form a new administration. As the Queen's 12th Prime Minister, he did so in alliance with the Liberal Democrats, thus forming the first, and perhaps only, coalition government of the reign.

The following month, as a reminder – if one were needed – that the Queen is not only head of state in the United Kingdom, Her Majesty made her 23rd visit to Canada. Almost 60 years after the then Princess Elizabeth and the Duke of Edinburgh undertook their first tour in the autumn of 1951, the Queen's 2010 visit – or 'homecoming' as Canadians prefer to think of it – was made primarily to celebrate the centenary of the Royal Canadian Navy and to mark Canada Day. The trip included visits to Nova Scotia, Ottawa, Winnipeg and Toronto.

It was on arrival at the Garrison Grounds at the foot of the historic Halifax Citadel on 28 June, a day of brisk winds and torrential rain, that in response to her welcome, the Queen told her appreciative audience, 'My mother once said that this country felt like a home away from home for the Queen of Canada. I am delighted to report that it still does…'

On the second afternoon of their eight-day tour, in which the indefatigable 84-year-old sovereign and her 89-year-old husband undertook 12-hour days of official engagements, the review and celebration of the Royal Canadian Navy took place off the coast of Halifax. Taking part in the impressive flotilla, consisting of coastguard vessels and 28 warships, were eight of the world's navies, among them the British, French and American.

The Queen's Diamond Jubilee 181

THE PRESENT DAY

Canada Day in Ottawa on 1 July once again provided the Queen with the opportunity to pay tribute to Canadians when, to cheers and whistles from the thousands of spectators on Parliament Hill, she said, 'During my lifetime, I have been a witness to this country for more than half its history since confederation. I have watched with enormous admiration how Canada has grown and matured, while remaining true to its history, its distinctive character and its values.'

Five days later, the Queen and Prince Philip flew out of Toronto at the end of their tour *en route* to New York, where Her Majesty addressed the General Assembly of the United Nations. It was the first time she had done so since 1957 when, just five years into her reign, she had expressed a guarded optimism about the UN's ability to realise the aims of its founding fathers. Fifty-three years later, she praised the organisation as 'a real force for common good'. Speaking 'as Queen of 16 United Nations member states and as Head of the Commonwealth of 54 countries', Her Majesty referred to issues of pressing global concern, including climate change and world peace. But, she said, 'new challenges have also emerged which have tested this organisation as much as its member states. One such is the struggle against terrorism…'

It was the undiminished memory of the devastating terrorist attack on the World Trade Center on 11 September 2001 that then, appropriately, took the Queen from the Upper East Side to Lower Manhattan. Following a wreath-laying ceremony at Ground Zero, she met representatives of the emergency services and Americans who had lost family members when the Twin Towers were targeted.

From there, the Queen drove a few blocks further south to the junction of Wall Street and Hanover Square, where she formally opened the British Garden. Created as a memorial to the 67 Britons who were killed on 9/11, the garden – in the shape of the British Isles – is paved with Caithness and Moray stone, imported from Scotland, and planted with trees and winding boxwood hedges. As at Ground Zero, and despite sweltering temperatures of 103 degrees, the Queen and Prince Philip took time to talk informally with some of the relatives of those who had died. In 2005, during their own visit to New York, the Prince of Wales and the Duchess of Cornwall had unveiled the garden's centre stone, while a little over a year before his grandmother's visit, Prince Harry had planted a tree during the garden's official naming ceremony.

Back home not long afterwards, the Queen and Prince Philip, together with several members of their family, set sail from Stornoway, on the Isle of Lewis, for a 10-day cruise of the Western Isles, before travelling on to Balmoral.

Until 1997, when she was decommissioned, the Royal Yacht *Britannia* had always taken the Queen on a cruise up the west coast. Now, it fell to the *Hebridean Princess*, a former Caledonian MacBrayne ferry, which the Queen had first chartered for an 80th birthday cruise four years earlier, to fulfil that function. Described as 'more like an opulent country house hotel' than a ship, she followed the familiar route to islands, coves and secluded beaches enjoyed by the royal family that had once been taken by *Britannia*. During the voyage, there were also celebrations marking the milestone birthdays of Prince Andrew, Duke of York, who had reached 50 five months earlier on 19 February, and Anne, the Princess Royal, whose 60th birthday on 15 August was just a few weeks away.

Never entirely free of official responsibility, even when off duty, the Queen interrupted her holiday at Balmoral on 16 September to travel to Edinburgh where, at the Palace of Holyroodhouse, she welcomed Pope Benedict XVI to Scotland at the start of his four-day papal visit to the United Kingdom. Later in the year, before the Queen and Prince Philip set off on a five-day state visit to Oman and the United Arab Emirates, their first to that part of the world in over 30 years, a personal announcement was made. The world learnt that their second eldest grandson, Prince William of Wales, was to marry his long-term girlfriend Catherine Middleton, the elder daughter of self-made millionaires Michael and Carole Middleton. It was an engagement that had been in the making since the couple met eight years earlier and which had long been expected within the royal family.

'It is brilliant news,' the Queen told one guest at a reception she was hosting at Windsor Castle for leaders and representatives of British overseas territories. 'It has taken them a very long time.'

CHAPTER 9

The Queen's Diamond Jubilee

THE PRESENT DAY

Facing a barrage of flashbulbs and television lights at a photocall for the world's media at St James's Palace, Catherine proudly displayed her iconic sapphire and diamond engagement ring, the very one given to William's mother almost 30 years earlier.

With the focus now firmly on family events, the year 2010 drew to a close with the news that the Queen and the Duke of Edinburgh had become great-grandparents. On 29 December, a daughter had been born to their eldest grandson Peter Phillips and his Canadian wife Autumn. Born at the Royal Gloucester Hospital and weighing 8lbs 8oz, the baby, who was named Savannah, was christened three months later at the church of the Holy Cross in the Cotswold village of Avening, near Gatcombe Park, the private estate of her grandmother, the Princess Royal.

With the approach of spring, mounting interest in the April wedding of Prince William and Kate Middleton threatened to be eclipsed by the less welcome, though entirely valid, media attention that engulfed the Queen's second son, Prince Andrew. Over five intense days in March, the press not only led on the Duke of York's long-standing friendship with Jeffrey Epstein, an American billionaire financier and convicted paedophile, but also questioned his judgement as Britain's Special

184 The Queen's Diamond Jubilee

Representative for International Trade and Investment. He would finally relinquish this title five months later. His alleged association with a number of controversial individuals, among them Saif Gaddafi, son of the despotic Libyan leader, Tarek Kaituni, a Libyan convicted of arms smuggling, and the son-in-law of Tunisia's ousted president Zine al-Abidine Ben Ali, whom the Duke had entertained at Buckingham Palace, proved too much for the Palace and the public to tolerate.

Revelations about Prince Andrew also extended to the behaviour of his former wife, Sarah Ferguson, who was again to be found millions of pounds in debt, indulging in tearful self-pity on American television, and offering to sell introductions to her ex-husband for cash in hand. Unedifying though the reports and allegations were, the feeding frenzy abated, slipping from the headlines and leader columns, to be replaced by more attractive, if more everyday, stories.

One such was the traditional Easter ritual of Royal Maundy (the day before Good Friday), which in 2011 fell on 21 April, by coincidence the Queen's 85th birthday. That morning the ceremony, which at Her Majesty's instigation takes place at a different cathedral each year, was celebrated at Westminster Abbey. An adapted form of an ancient ceremony known in England since the 7th century, it has its origins in the Last Supper, when Christ, having washed the feet of His Disciples, gave them the command – or '*mandatum*', from which the word 'Maundy' is derived – to love one another.

In past centuries, it not only fell to the monarch to wash the feet of a chosen number of poor, but also to distribute to them gifts of food and clothing. With the passage of time, those rituals were dispensed with and food and clothing were replaced by gifts of Maundy Money.

So it was that Her Majesty distributed two leather purses to 85 men and 85 women, the white one containing 85 pence in Maundy coins and the red one containing a £5 coin to mark Prince Philip's 90th birthday and a London 2012 Olympic Games 50 pence piece. As custom decrees, the number of recipients each year corresponds with the sovereign's age.

Eight days later, on 29 April, Westminster Abbey became the focus of world attention as an estimated television audience of two billion people in 180 countries – including 24 million in the UK alone – joined one million flag-waving spectators packed along the processional route to celebrate the wedding of Prince William – or, as he had just become, the Duke of Cambridge, Earl of Strathearn and Baron Carrickfergus – and Catherine Middleton.

With the country barely out of recession, however, and stringent austerity measures being implemented by the government, the wedding, while not diminishing the importance of the occasion – was the first royal wedding at Westminster Abbey since that of Prince Andrew and Sarah Ferguson in 1986 and the most significant since William's parents were married 30 years earlier. It was expected to reflect the restrained mood of the times.

THE PRESENT DAY

While there was little extravagance for anyone to complain about, it was an occasion of splendour, romance and sheer happiness that was best summed up by the Queen who, on her return to Buckingham Palace, was heard to remark, 'It was amazing'. And so it was. A wedding that combined the traditional with the contemporary, the expected with the sometimes unexpected, it was inevitably made up of myriad memorable moments. The bride's arrival, to a cacophony of cheers and pealing bells, provided the first proper look at her exquisite lace and satin gazar wedding dress, designed by Sarah Burton of Alexander McQueen. Its skirt and train were appliquéd with delicate lace flowers – roses, shamrocks, daffodils and thistles, the floral emblems of the United Kingdom – which had been painstakingly made by hand at the Royal School of Needlework at Hampton Court.

Inside Westminster Abbey, scented by 30,000 flowers in shades of white, cream and green, six 20ft white flowering English field maples placed on either side of the nave created the impression, perhaps intentionally, of a leafy path to a country village church. At the steps of the sacrarium, which contains the magnificent and recently restored 13th-century Cosmati Pavement, the new Duke of Cambridge, who only two months earlier had been appointed Colonel of the Irish Guards, was dressed for the first time in the Irish Guards mounted officer's uniform in guard of honour order. Across his scarlet tunic – constructed for him by uniform makers Kashket and Partners from special heat-absorbing material to prevent him passing out under the heat of the television lights – he wore the blue riband of the Order of the Garter, together with the Garter Star, the wings of the RAF and the Golden Jubilee Medal.

This new uniform, together with bearskin, would be worn again by William five weeks later when he took part in the Trooping the Colour ceremony for the first time. Standing next to him, however, as he awaited the arrival of his bride, was Prince Harry, his best man, a captain in the Blues and Royals, whose ceremonial uniform he wore.

THE PRESENT DAY

An hour later, after the exchange of vows, which was greeted with cheers and applause from the crowds outside, to whom the service was relayed, William and Catherine, who had now become Her Royal Highness The Duchess of Cambridge, bowed and curtsied respectively to the Queen, before making their way to the West Door. From there, the crimson and gold 1902 State Landau, drawn by four of the famous Windsor Greys and accompanied by a Captain's Escort of the Household Cavalry, waited to take them to Buckingham Palace. Following them, Prince Harry and the bride's sister Pippa, who as maid of honour had made quite an impression in her slender, figure-hugging ivory dress, each travelled in an Ascot landau with the young bridesmaids and pages, the latter splendidly dressed in replicas of a Grenadier Guards officer's uniform of the 1820s.

Other lasting impressions of an altogether memorable occasion included the moment the bride and bridegroom stepped on to the palace balcony to acknowledge the ocean of cheering people, stretching away into the distance as far as the eye could see. 'Oh wow!' the new Duchess exclaimed, before she and her husband satisfied public expectation and

188   The Queen's Diamond Jubilee

CHAPTER 9

exchanged not one but two kisses.

Less than a week later – their honeymoon in the Seychelles had to wait a while – nothing could have been further removed from the pageantry of their wedding day as William went back to work at RAF Valley in Anglesey, where he was among the crew of a Sea King helicopter that carried out a double mountain rescue in Snowdonia. Catherine, meanwhile, still insisting on a no-nonsense, no staff, home life – which meant cooking William's evening meals herself – was seen with her shopping trolley at the local Waitrose supermarket. It was an indication of how, at least for the present, this well-grounded and unpretentious royal couple, the principal representatives of tomorrow's monarchy, want to manage their lives.

Thursday 12 May, apart from being the 54th anniversary of her parents' coronation in 1937, was much like any another day in the Queen's diary, except that it was the day on which she attained the distinction of becoming Britain's second-longest-reigning sovereign. Only Queen Victoria has reigned longer, 63 years and 7 months, and that is a record it seems very likely her great-great-granddaughter will surpass on 10 September 2015.

The Queen's Diamond Jubilee 189

THE PRESENT DAY

Historic though that particular milestone was, another of far greater political significance occurred the following week when, accompanied by Prince Philip, the Queen became the first British sovereign to visit the Republic of Ireland.

Only a generation ago such a visit would have been inconceivable. But following the 1998 Good Friday Agreement, the prospect, although considered by some to still be too soon, was fostered by Ireland's president, Mary McAleese (the theme of whose presidency was 'building bridges') and became viable.

Even so, during the four-day visit from 17 to 20 May nothing was left to chance and therefore the security operation was unprecedented, even stifling. In central Dublin, where 25 miles of steel barriers were erected round the city, 8,000 police officers, plain-clothes detectives and soldiers were deployed on the ground, with marksmen on rooftops and helicopters overhead. Everywhere she went, through all but deserted streets, the Queen travelled in an armour-plated Range Rover.

In a visit that was inevitably going to be imbued with symbolism of one kind or another almost at every turn, the

CHAPTER 9

Queen's choice of emerald green coat (described officially as 'jade') and hat struck the right note as she alighted from her aircraft at Casement military airbase. Greeted by the British Ambassador, the Queen then drove to Phoenix Park where, at Áras an Uachtaráin, once the Vice-Regal Lodge, she was welcomed by President McAleese.

Scarcely three hours later, the Queen undertook what was perhaps the single most important – and certainly profoundly appreciated – engagement of the entire visit. In what was a deeply significant act of reconciliation – as well as a stark reminder of the very darkest days of Ireland's struggle to break free from British rule – the Queen, with President McAleese, drove to Dublin's Garden of Remembrance in Parnell Square. Opened in 1966, it remembered the patriots who died for Ireland or, put less gently, it commemorated the Irish rebels who were executed by the British Crown. Having laid a wreath, the Queen stepped back and bowed her head, observing a solemn one-minute silence. That act was intended to be a healing gesture and to most people it conveyed a message that was beyond words.

Next day, as a counterbalance to the deeper moments, the Queen and her husband visited the Guinness Storehouse, one of Ireland's main tourist attractions, where a pint of the national brew was pulled and placed on the counter to allow it to settle. There were light-hearted exchanges, plenty of smiles and a keen eye or two trained on the world-famous dry stout, but neither of the royal visitors, doubtless to the disappointment of some, picked the glass up.

Returning to the more poignant engagements on the itinerary, further acts of respect and remembrance took the Queen and Prince Philip first to the Irish National War Memorial Park at Islandbridge, where the almost 50,000 soldiers who had given their lives during the Great War – most of them fighting with the British – are commemorated. They also visited Croke Park, the Gaelic Athletic Association's major football ground; the scene of the original 'Bloody Sunday', it was there on 21 November 1920 that British forces opened fire on a crowd of football supporters in retaliation for the assassination by the IRA of 14 British intelligence officers. Fourteen civilians, the youngest of whom were aged 10 and 11, lost their lives and 65 more were injured.

THE PRESENT DAY

That evening, together with the Duke of Edinburgh, the Queen, wearing a long white dress designed by Angela Kelly that was appliquéd with over 2,000 silk shamrocks and sewn with an Irish harp made of Swarovski crystals, attended a state dinner in St Patrick's Hall at Dublin Castle.

To general surprise, the Queen began her speech with a few words in Irish: '*A Uachtaráin agus a chairde*' – 'President and friends'. It was a gesture that had President McAleese quietly but clearly saying 'Wow', no fewer than three times, and which earned appreciative applause from everyone else. On such occasions, it is exactly the sort of diplomatic touch that matters.

Moving on, it was the past as much as the future that the Queen addressed when she said that while Ireland and Britain had much in common, it was 'impossible to ignore the weight of history'.

'With the benefit of historical hindsight,' she said, 'we can all see things which we would wish had been done differently or not at all.'

As one observer put it afterwards, 'those words were received with considerable gratitude… coming as they did from a respected British monarch [and representing] a sensitive but dignified acceptance of past wrongs'.

Leaving Dublin, the Queen had the opportunity to indulge her passion as a horse owner and breeder when she visited the Irish National Stud in County Kildare. Relaxed and in animated conversation with trainers and breeders, she was delighted to meet jockeys who had ridden the famous steeplechaser Arkle in the 1960s. She was no less pleased to have the opportunity of speaking with 87-year-old T. P. Burns, who once rode winners for the Queen Mother.

Perhaps the most unusual gift the Queen was given during her four-day visit to Ireland, however, came from Christina Patino, who has horses stabled at the breeding centre. She offered a visit by one of the Queen's mares to a stallion named Big Bad Bob, a meeting that would usually cost over £5,000 in stud fees. Should she take up the offer, it would not be the first time the Queen had sent horses to the Irish National Stud to breed. Indeed, General Synod, one of the most promising colts in her stable in 2011, was sired by Invincible Spirit, one of the stallions she saw during her visit.

As the Queen left Ireland on 20 May, none but the most hardened of republicans would have denied that it had been a profoundly important and highly successful state visit, one that would long be remembered.

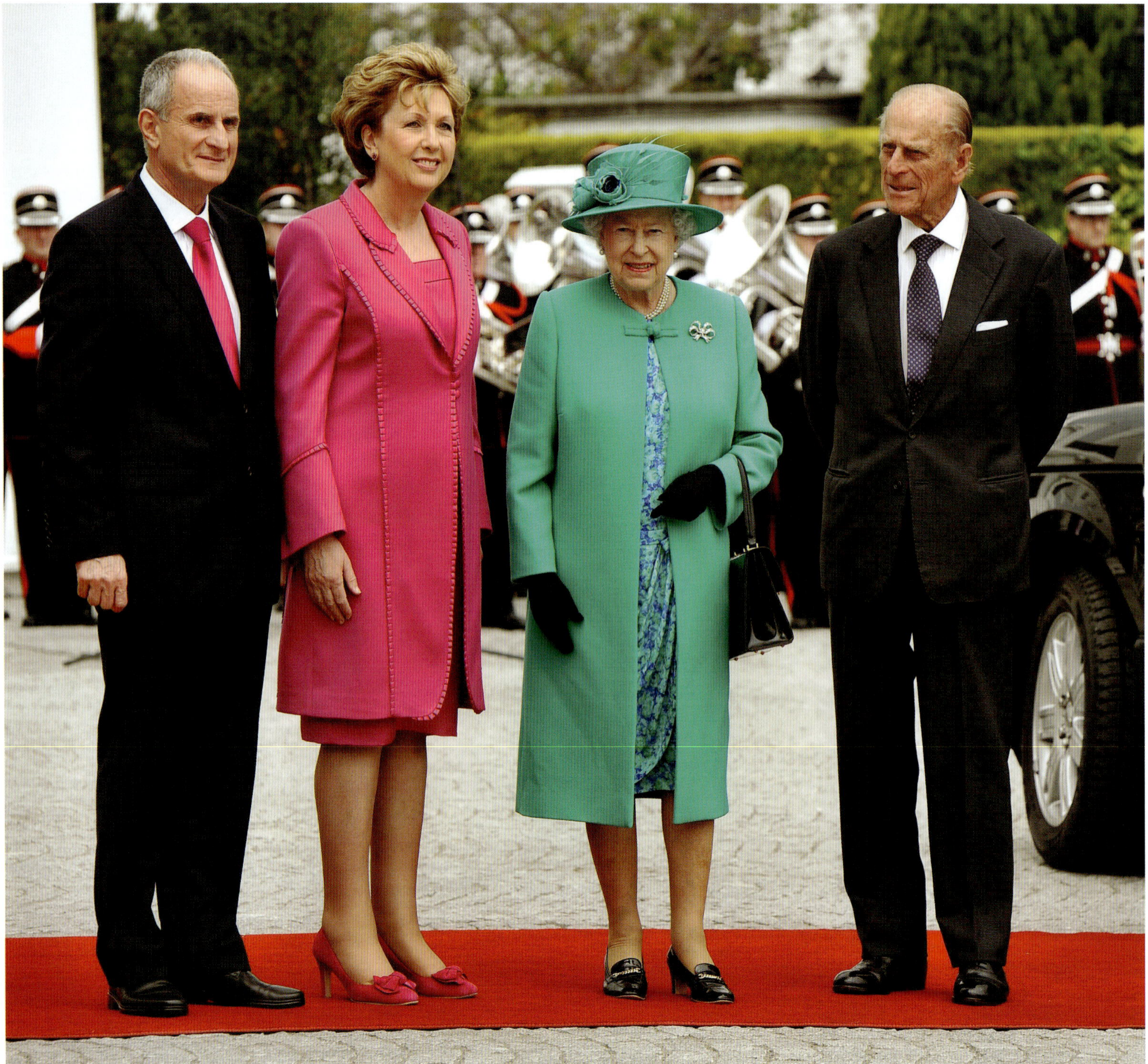

Exchanging the role of guest for that of host, the Queen had barely had chance to draw breath before she and Prince Philip received the United States President Barack Obama and his wife Michelle, at the start of their own state visit.

They had, of course, met before and, as on that occasion two years earlier, there was a distinct sense of warmth and cordiality between the couples. At the glittering state banquet at Buckingham Palace on the first evening, there was, inevitably, specific mention of the 'special relationship', now apparently upgraded to 'essential', that continues to exist between Britain and America. Indeed, the very nature of the visit was to reaffirm 'one of the oldest, one of the strongest alliances the world has ever known', with Mr Obama, the 12th US president of Her Majesty's reign, quoting Winston Churchill's 'union of hearts based on convictions and common ideals'.

Deeper political issues concerning the state of the world's economy, overseas military involvement in Afghanistan and elsewhere, and other matters involving the two countries' shared interests, had, of course, to wait for another day. But celebrating the fact that the United States, as the Queen put it, 'remains our most important ally' – and presumably vice-versa – ensured that the stated reaffirmation agenda of the visit had got off to exactly the right start.

THE PRESENT DAY

196 The Queen's Diamond Jubilee

At the time of their Golden Wedding anniversary in 1997, it will be remembered that the Queen said of the man she had married 50 years earlier, 'He is someone who doesn't take easily to compliments.' Fourteen years further on in time, that sentiment, as Prince Philip reached his 90th birthday on 10 June 2011, was no less apposite, with the Prince himself telling Fiona Bruce, in one of two at times awkward and typically irascible television interviews that he gave, 'I reckon I've done my bit. I want to enjoy myself… with less responsibility, less rushing about… less trying to think of something to say.' The Prince continued that he now intended to wind down and cut back on his usual tally of 300 official engagements each year. That, however, is difficult for many an active, still curious, still questioning nonagenarian, let alone somebody like Prince Philip, who mentally as well as physically is rarely still. It is something that remains to be seen.

In fact, even his 90th birthday was a working day, with a function for the Action on Hearing Loss charity in the morning and, as has long been something of a tradition the night before Trooping the Colour, hosting a dinner for the senior colonels of the Household Division at Buckingham Palace. On the Sunday, ahead of Garter Day and Ascot Week, there was a private service – Matins – at St George's Chapel, Windsor Castle, which he and the Queen attended with their family and more than 700 guests.

During the service, in which the Dean of Windsor, the Right Rev David Conner, delivered a humorous address, the choir performed the *Jubilate Deo* with music by Benjamin Britten, in a setting that Prince Philip himself had requested for St George's Day 50 years before in 1961.

In tribute and as her own special gift to her husband, one that friends say touched him deeply, the Queen conferred upon Prince Philip the honour of Lord High Admiral. That office, as titular head of the Royal Navy, which the Queen herself had held since 1964, when the Senior Service's organisational structure was reviewed and the title re-invested in the sovereign, dates back to the 14th century, when the English Navy was consolidated into one force.

Before the Queen and Prince Philip's traditional annual holiday at Balmoral came around once again, and in advance of the start of their autumn schedule, which would take them to Australia – their 16th and very probably their last long-haul visit – for the Commonwealth Heads of Government Meeting in Perth, there was one more private family celebration to be attended. That, on 30 July, a brilliantly sunny day in Edinburgh, was the wedding of their eldest granddaughter Zara Phillips and the England rugby player Mike Tindall at Canongate Kirk.

Though regarded as a private, family occasion, it still drew crowds, who packed into the limited space available outside the church to watch the arrival of royal and celebrity guests, most of them sports personalities. And of course, to cheer the bride herself, who, wearing a dress of ivory silk faille by Stewart Parvin, one of the Queen's favourite designers, and a diamond Greek key tiara once owned by Prince Philip's mother, arrived from the Palace of Holyroodhouse with her father. Two days later – like William and Catherine, the honeymoon had to wait – it was back to work for the newly married couple, with Zara, as an international three-day eventer, preparing for the launch of her own line of children's equestrian clothing and taking part in the annual Festival of British Eventing at Gatcombe Park. Mike Tindall went back to training in Surrey for his next international match, an England versus Wales friendly at Twickenham.

THE PRESENT DAY

For Queen Elizabeth II, the next major 'fixture' in her official diary is the Diamond Jubilee, when the nation and the Commonwealth will celebrate the 60th anniversary of her accession to the throne. Over an extended bank holiday weekend in June, during which 2012 beacons – or bonfires – will be lit throughout the United Kingdom, a 'Big Jubilee Lunch' held and a celebratory concert staged at Buckingham Palace, the Queen will take part in a pageant on the River Thames. Travelling aboard a royal barge, inspired by those of the 17th and 18th centuries and specially constructed from a working sailing barge, she will lead a spectacular flotilla of 1,000 vessels up the Thames from Putney to Tower Bridge. St Paul's Cathedral will be the setting for a service of thanksgiving, as it was for the Silver and Golden Jubilees in 1977 and 2002.

It will, of course, be an occasion when tributes of all kinds and every description will be paid to the Queen from around the globe. Through 60 often turbulent and inevitably changing years, Her Majesty has remained a reassuringly constant figure, not just at home but on the world stage. Her Diamond Jubilee will be a time for appreciative reflection and of course celebration of a life and reign that, in the fullness of time, will be difficult to follow.

CHAPTER 9

The Queen's Diamond Jubilee

CHAPTER 10

Sixty Glorious Years

by JOE LITTLE

QUEEN VICTORIA WAS the first British monarch to celebrate a Diamond Jubilee. 'How well I remember this day sixty years ago,' she recorded in her journal on 20 June 1897, 'when I was called from my bed by dear Mama to receive the news of my accession.'

Because the 78-year-old Queen was by now frail, it was decided that her Diamond Jubilee celebrations would not be on the same scale as those marking her Golden Jubilee 10 years earlier. Westminster Abbey had been the venue for an inspiring service of thanksgiving in 1887, but a decade later Her Majesty felt that something similar would be too arduous for her. Consequently a smaller but nevertheless impressive celebration (of no more than 20 minutes' duration, she instructed) was devised for St Paul's Cathedral. And so on 22 June a service was held on the steps outside because Queen Victoria was too weak to climb them into the great building.

Excerpts from her journals reveal exactly how the Queen perceived – and coped with – the festivities marking her long reign.

The Queen's Diamond Jubilee 201

20 June 1897

'This eventful day, 1897, has opened, and I pray God to help and protect me as He has hitherto done during those 60 long eventful years!

'At eleven I, with my family, went to St George's Chapel, where a short touching service took place... The service began with the hymn, *Now Thank We All Our God*, followed by some of the usual morning prayers.

'Dear Albert's beautiful *Te Deum* was sung, and the special prayer for Accession Day followed, with a few others. Felt rather nervous about the coming days, and that all should go off well.'

As the last notes of the organ died away, all the family rose to their feet and, led by the Empress Frederick, Victoria's eldest child, they walked over to the Queen, kissing her affectionately. Her Majesty also visited Prince Albert's tomb in the mausoleum at Frogmore and 'remained sitting there some little time'.

21 June 1897

'The 10th anniversary of the celebration of my fifty years Jubilee. Breakfasted with my three daughters at the Cottage at Frogmore. A fine warm morning.

'At quarter to twelve we drove to the station to start for London. The town was very prettily decorated, and there were great crowds, who cheered very much... Then we proceeded at a slow trot, with a Sovereign's escort of the 1st Life Guards. Passed through dense crowds [between Paddington Station and Buckingham Palace], who gave me a most enthusiastic reception. It was like a triumphal entry... The windows, the roofs of the houses, were one mass of beaming faces, and the cheers never ceased.

'On entering the park, through the Marble Arch, the crowd was even greater, carriages were drawn up amongst the people on foot, even on the pretty little lodges well-dressed people were perched. Hyde Park Corner and Constitution Hill were densely crowded. All vied with one another to give me a heartfelt, loyal, and affectionate welcome. I was deeply touched and gratified. The day had become very fine and very hot.

'Reached the palace shortly after 1… I was taken round in my wheeled chair to the Bow Room, where all my family awaited me, including Marie Coburg [her daughter-in-law, the wife of Prince Alfred], whom I had not yet seen. Seated in my chair, as I cannot stand long, I received all the foreign Princes in succession, beginning with the Archduke Franz Ferdinand [heir to the Austrian throne, who was assassinated at Sarajevo in 1914].

'Dressed for dinner. I wore a dress of which the whole front was embroidered in gold, which had been specially worked in India, diamonds in my cap, and a diamond necklace, etc. The dinner was in the Supper-room at little tables of twelve each. All the family, foreign royalties, special Ambassadors and Envoys were invited. I sat between the Archduke Franz Ferdinand and the Prince of Naples.

SIXTY GLORIOUS YEARS

204　The Queen's Diamond Jubilee

'After dinner went into Ball-room, where my private band played and the following were presented to me: the Colonial Premiers with their wives, the Special Envoys, the three Indian Princes, and all the officers of the two Indian escorts, who, as usual, held out their swords to be touched by me, and the different foreign suites.

'The Ball-room was very full and dreadfully hot, and the lighting very inefficient. It was only a little after eleven when I got back to my room, feeling very tired. There was a deal of noise in the streets, and we were told that many were sleeping out in the parks.'

Much to his chagrin, Kaiser Wilhelm II, Victoria's eldest grandchild, was not invited; it had been decided that in contrast to the 1887 jubilee this would be a more low-key affair with no foreign heads of state present. At the suggestion of Joseph Chamberlain, the Colonial Secretary, the emphasis was very much on the size and might of the British Empire.

22 June 1897

'A never-to-be-forgotten day. No one ever, I believe, has met with such an ovation as was given to me passing through those six miles of streets… The crowds were quite indescribable, and their enthusiasm truly marvellous and deeply touching. The cheering was quite deafening, and every face seemed to be filled with real joy.

'The night had been very hot, and I was rather restless. There was such a noise going on the whole time, but it did not keep me from getting some sleep. Dull early and close. Breakfasted with Vicky, Lenchen and Beatrice in the Chinese luncheon room. The head of the procession, including the Colonial troops, had unfortunately already passed the palace before I got to breakfast, but there were still a great many, chiefly British, passing by. I watched them for a little while.

'At a quarter-past eleven, the others being seated in their carriages long before, and having preceded me a short distance, I started from the State entrance in an open State landau, drawn by eight creams. Dear Alix, looking very pretty in lilac, and Lenchen sat opposite me. I felt a good deal agitated, and had been so all these days, for fear anything might be forgotten or go wrong…

'Before leaving I touched an electric button, by which I started a message which was telegraphed throughout the whole Empire. It was the following: "From my heart I thank our beloved people, May God bless them!" At this time the sun burst out. Vicky was in the carriage nearest me, not being able to go in mine, as her rank as Empress prevented her sitting with her back to the horses, for I had to sit alone. Her carriage was drawn by four blacks, richly caparisoned in red…

'The denseness of the crowds was immense, but the order maintained wonderful. The streets in the Strand are now quite wide, but one misses Temple Bar. Here the Lord Mayor received me and presented the sword, which I touched. He then immediately mounted his horse in his robes, and galloped past bare-headed [his hat having flown off], carrying the sword, preceding my carriage, accompanied by his Sheriffs. As we neared St Paul's the procession was often stopped, and the crowds broke out into singing *God Save the Queen*. In one house were assembled the survivors of the Battle of Balaclava.

'In front of the Cathedral the scene was most impressive. All the Colonial troops, on foot, were drawn up round the Square. My carriage, surrounded by all the Royal Princes, was drawn up close to the steps, where the Clergy were assembled, the Bishops in rich copes, with their crosiers, the Archbishop of Canterbury and the Bishop of London each holding a very fine one. A *Te Deum* was sung…

'[On returning to Buckingham Palace] I stopped in front of the Mansion House, where the Lady Mayoress presented me with a beautiful silver basket full of orchids. Here I took leave of the Lord Mayor. Both he and the Lady Mayoress were quite *émus* [moved].

'Got home at a quarter to two. Had a quiet luncheon with Vicky, Beatrice and her three children. Troops continually passing by. Then rested and later had tea with Lenchen in the garden. There was a large dinner in the Supper-room.'

The stands erected outside the cathedral for officials and other guests had been tested for stability by 250 men of the City of London police. They were made to march and counter-march over the seats, ascending and descending the steps all at the same time. It had been suggested that the statue of Queen Anne in the cathedral forecourt might block the view of spectators – royal or otherwise – and that it should be removed. Queen Victoria was horrified at the thought, protesting loudly, 'Move Queen Anne? One day someone might suggest moving me instead.'

One very observant participant in her grandmother's Diamond Jubilee celebrations was 14-year-old Princess Alice of Albany, the only daughter of Prince Leopold, Duke of Albany, Queen Victoria's fourth and youngest son. Later, as Princess Alice, Countess of Athlone, she would outlive all of Queen Victoria's grandchildren.

Reminiscing many years later in her charming memoirs, *For My Grandchildren,* the Princess gave a detailed account of what for her would always be a day quite unlike any other.

'Grandmama Victoria's Diamond Jubilee was the most historic of the many royal pageants I have attended, for hers was the longest reign of any British sovereign. It occurred when the Empire was reaching its greatest extent and the summit of its power. The date was June 22nd, 1897, when the Queen had been on the throne for exactly sixty years and was to remain on it for nearly four more – thus making her reign the longest in our history.

'The day, I remember, began by being overcast, but by time the procession was due to leave Buckingham Palace the clouds had cleared away and the sun continued to shine until the Queen returned exactly three hours later. As she was nearing her eightieth year there was considerable anxiety as to her ability to stand the strain, but she withstood the ordeal wonderfully without ever relaxing her animation, though at times it was very hot in the carriages.

'She wore a dress and mantle of her customary black silk embroidered for the occasion with silver. Her bonnet was also of black lace trimmed with a wreath of white acacia and ornamented with an aigrette of diamonds. The only touch of colour was provided by the blue Sash and Star of the Garter. She wisely carried a parasol of white lace which she used to protect herself from the hot sun. Her open carriage was drawn by eight cream-coloured horses ridden by postilions with red-coated footmen at their sides. She was accompanied by Aunt

Alix, Princess of Wales, who wore a beautiful mauve dress trimmed with lace and a bonnet of similar colour with mauve flowers. Uncle Bertie, Prince of Wales, rode beside her carriage looking magnificent in his Field-Marshal's uniform. Uncle Arthur of Connaught, then General Officer commanding the troops, and Uncle George Cambridge also rode beside her carriage. Many foreign princes rode in the procession and others were in carriages.

'Aunt Vicky, Empress of Germany, and Uncle Alfred, Duke of Saxe-Coburg-Gotha, rode in the carriage immediately preceding the Queen's and Mother [the Duchess of Albany] rode in the next carriage with Uncle Alfred's Duchess Aunt Marie and Aunt Louischen of Connaught.

'My brother Charlie, then Duke of Albany [later Duke of Coburg], was in a carriage with several of his cousins, including Margaret of Connaught. I was one carriage away from them in the charge of the Duchess of Buccleuch, Mistress of the Robes, accompanied by the Battenburg girls, Ena and Alice.

'Charlie and Drino Carisbrooke, having spent the morning on the palace roof watching the Colonial troops, came down and gulped a hurried breakfast before getting into their carriage. In consequence, when the sun came out, Charlie suddenly felt he had to be sick and I remember a St John's ambulance drew up and he was taken inside to be relieved of his hasty meal. Ena, afterwards Queen of Spain, was very excited, and her gaiety and pretty looks attracted the attention of the crowds.

'Behind us we could hear the deafening roar as the vast crowds cheered the Queen, who was, of course, the centre of attention.

The Queen's Diamond Jubilee 207

SIXTY GLORIOUS YEARS

208 The Queen's Diamond Jubilee

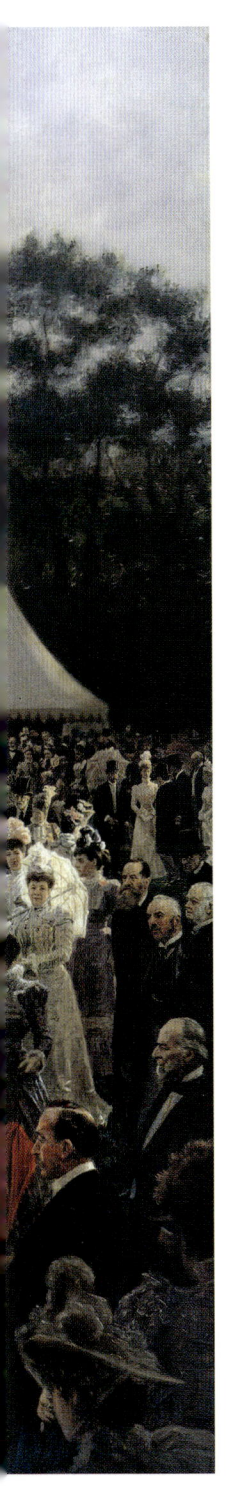

'We got into our carriages at the palace and I caught a glimpse of Aunt Vicky looking from one of the windows as she waited for hers. I also noted that the roofs were crowded with spectators. The procession was headed by regiments from various parts of the Empire, including Canadians, Australians, New Zealanders, Indians and contingents of African and West Indian units blending together to produce a unique and picturesque display. I was especially interested in the Fijians with their hair trained upwards and dyed a reddish colour.

'Behind them rode the Premiers of the Colonies (the name "Dominion" was not in use then) headed by Sir William Laurier of Canada. As a compliment to the importance attached to the Empire their troops were under the command of Field Marshal Lord Roberts V.C. They received a tremendous ovation from the crowd as they marched past.

'The British troops were headed by Ossie Ames, the tallest man in the Army – and the stupidest. The streets were lined throughout the route by troops of the Guards and the Line Regiments. The Household Cavalry, including the Life Guards and the Dragoon Guards, escorted the royal procession.

'The route we followed was from Buckingham Palace to Hyde Park Corner; then along Piccadilly; down St James's Street into Pall Mall and Trafalgar Square, which was lined on all sides by the Royal Navy and the Royal Marines. Then we entered the Strand, where the Lord Mayor was waiting to receive the Queen *en route* to St Paul's, where the commemoration service was to take place.

'The Mayor, who was riding a spirited charger, was clad in his flowing robes of state and wearing his chain of office – a quaint attire for a mounted man! I was told afterwards that he performed the immemorial ceremony of presenting the Sword of State to the Queen *on foot* and caused much merriment when he remounted his mettlesome steed – no mean feat for a man swathed in the cumbersome mayoral robes!

'The steps of St Paul's were crowded with members of the Diplomatic Corps from the embassies of the whole world and with richly clad rajahs and picturesque oriental dignitaries. Here the Queen was received by the Archbishops of Canterbury and York and the Prime Minister, Lord Salisbury, and other Ministers. The thanksgiving service took place on the steps of the Cathedral, ending with the crowd joining the choirs in singing *God Save the Queen*. The cheering which greeted Grandmama as she arrived and drove away was stupendous and deafening.

'The remainder of the route was down Cheapside and across London Bridge, evoking in all of us that sense of historic events which this ancient part of London always inspires.

'After a stop at the Mansion House, the cortège proceeded to the South Bank and returned over Westminster Bridge to the Speakers' Green, where the Members of Parliament were assembled to greet their Queen. I was told afterwards that she was deeply moved and impressed by the warmth of their reception.

'I understand that the Irish members, known then as the "Dillonites", who were fanatically demanding Home Rule, boycotted the ceremony, but it is more than likely that Grandmama was unaware of this protest, which was rather uncalled for on such a non-political occasion.

'The procession returned, via Pall Mall, to Buckingham Palace after an exciting three hours' journey through cheering crowds, the sound of the saluting guns in the park being scarcely audible above the enthusiastic clamour of the populace. The foreign visitors must have been profoundly impressed by this display of spontaneous loyalty.

'Grandmama was radiant throughout and did not seem in the least tired – probably owing to the stimulating effect of the demonstrations, the excitement of the experience and her gratitude for the devotion of her people. Although I have taken part in many impressive ceremonies, including several coronations, this was the most unforgettable event in my life.'

But as far as Queen Victoria was concerned, her Diamond Jubilee celebrations were far from over: during the next few weeks there were loyal addresses, receptions, loyal addresses, an awe-inspiring review of the fleet at Spithead, loyal addresses, garden parties at Buckingham Palace and Windsor Castle, and more loyal addresses. The final event, to Her Majesty's great relief, no doubt, took place on 15 July.

The Queen's Diamond Jubilee

PICTURE INDEX

CHAPTER 1:
THE EARLY YEARS

Page 6
PA.1161396. The christening of Princess Elizabeth, 29 May 1926. Back row, left to right: the Duke of Connaught, King George V, the Duke of York and the Earl of Strathmore. Front row: Lady Elphinstone, Queen Mary, the Duchess of York with Princess Elizabeth, the Countess of Strathmore and Princess Mary. Press Association Images.

Page 7
PA.1717253. The Duke and Duchess of York with their baby daughter, Princess Elizabeth, 29 April 1926. Press Association Images.

Page 8
PA.7153818. Princess Margaret Rose, 2, and Princess Elizabeth, 6, the Duke and Duchess of York's daughters, in London on 20 August 1934. Press Association Images.

Page 9
PA.1375920. The Duchess of York arrives at the Royal Tournament in London accompanied by Princess Elizabeth and Princess Margaret, 15 August 1935. Press Association Images.

Page 10
PA.7166909. From left: Miss Zoe d'Erlanger, Princess Margaret, the Master of Carnegie (later 3rd Duke of Fife), Princess Elizabeth, the Hon. Mary Anna Stunt and Master Robert Wolrige-Gordon attend the Master of Carnegie's sixth birthday party at Elsick House in Kincardineshire on 23 September 1935. Press Association Images.

Page 11
PA.1292826. Queen Elizabeth, Princess Elizabeth, Princess Margaret and King George VI on the balcony of Buckingham Palace after his coronation, 12 May 1937. Press Association Images.

Page 12
PA.1383079. Princess Elizabeth (right) and Princess Margaret after their broadcast on *Children's Hour* on 13 October 1940. Press Association Images.

Page 13
PA.1383080. Princess Elizabeth and Princess Margaret in the garden of their wartime country residence (Windsor) where they are staying. In view of the petrol shortage, Their Royal Highnesses' pony cart has again been brought into use. Press Association Images.

Page 14
PA.7154575. Princess Elizabeth, left, and Princess Margaret perform in *Cinderella* at Windsor Castle on 9 February 1942. They produced the show for the aid of the Royal Household Concerts' Wool Fund. AP/Press Association Images.

Page 15
PA.3422517. Princess Elizabeth and Princess Margaret, in their Girl Guide uniforms, practise their bandaging skills in this August 1943 file photo. Princess Elizabeth is wearing the badge of the Swallow Patrol and two white stripes, which indicates that she is patrol leader. AP/Press Association Images.

Page 16
PA.7494715. Queen Elizabeth and her daughters sit for a portrait by Cecil Beaton in the Bow Room at Buckingham Palace on 5 February 1943. Cecil Beaton/AP/Press Association Images.

Page 17
PA.7226922. Princess Elizabeth holds the bridle of one of the farm horses at Sandringham, the King's country home in Norfolk, on 16 April 1944. The Princess will be 18 years old on April 21 and will then officially come of age. AP/Press Association Images.

Page 18
PA.1409854. Princess Elizabeth receives vehicle maintenance instruction on an Austin 10 Light Utility Vehicle while serving with No. 1 M.T. Training Centre at Camberley, Surrey, in the spring of 1945. Imperial War Museum/AP/Press Association Images.

Page 19
PA.7184535. During ceremonies at No. 1 M.T. Training Centre at Camberley on 3 August 1945, Princess Elizabeth, a Junior Commander, ATS, received a clock from associates at the camp where she received her early training. AP/Press Association Images.

Page 20
PA.1412800. The King's daughters are bridesmaids at the wedding of the Hon. Patricia Mountbatten to Captain the Lord Brabourne. Here, arriving at Romsey Abbey, are George VI, Queen Elizabeth, Princess Elizabeth, Princess Margaret and Lieutenant Philip Mountbatten, 26 October 1946. Press Association Images.

Page 21
PA.7355542. Princess Margaret Rose, King George VI and Princess Elizabeth examine a book with Queen Elizabeth on 7 December 1946. AP/Press Association Images.

Page 22
PA.6060835. Princess Elizabeth arrives at the pavilion for the Crowning of the Bard at Mountain Ash, Glamorgan, Wales, on 6 August 1946. The Princess was made an honorary Ovate of the Welsh Gorsedd of Bards. AP/Press Association Images.

PA.7172332. A portrait of Princess Elizabeth taken on 7 December 1946. AP/Press Association Images.

Page 23
PA.1163974. An informal picture of King George VI and Princess Elizabeth during a visit to Natal National Park in South Africa, 22 March 1947. Press Association Images.

Page 24
PA.3410788. A specially posed portrait of Princess Elizabeth before the microphone for her 21st-birthday speech, which she made from Cape Town, South Africa, on 21 April 1947. AP/Press Association Images.

Page 25
PA.7259129. Princess Elizabeth, on her first appearance on horseback at an official ceremony, wears the uniform of a Colonel in the Grenadier Guards as she rides side-saddle back to Buckingham Palace on 12 June 1947 after attending the Trooping the Colour ceremony, King George VI's official birthday parade. AP/Press Association Images.

Page 26
PA.4472667, PA.1573102 and PA.4472684. The engagement of Princess Elizabeth to Lieutenant Philip Mountbatten is announced and the happy couple are pictured together at Buckingham Palace on 10 July 1947. Press Association Images.

Page 27
PA.10903791. Princess Elizabeth and Lieutenant Philip Mountbatten, RN receive a wedding present of an electric sewing machine on 31 October 1947 at Clydebank, where they launched the liner *Caronia*. Press Association Images.

CHAPTER 2: LOVE & MARRIAGE

Page 28
PA.4473111. Princess Elizabeth and the Duke of Edinburgh at Buckingham Palace after their wedding ceremony, 20 November 1947.
Press Association Images.

Page 30
PA.4472769. Princess Elizabeth and the Duke of Edinburgh with close relatives and bridesmaids in the Throne Room at Buckingham Palace immediately after their wedding ceremony, 20 November 1947. Front row, left to right: Queen Mary, Princess Alice of Greece, Prince William of Gloucester with fellow pageboy Prince Michael of Kent, King George VI and Queen Elizabeth, and the Dowager Marchioness of Milford Haven (Philip's grandmother). Back row: the Hon. Margaret Elphinstone, Lady Pamela Mountbatten, Lady Mary Cambridge, Princess Alexandra of Kent, Princess Margaret, Lady Caroline Montagu-Douglas-Scott, Lady Elizabeth Lambart and the Hon. Diana Bowes Lyon. Press Association Images.

Page 31
PA.1185794. Princess Elizabeth and the Duke of Edinburgh set off in a carriage procession to Waterloo Station for their train to Winchester at the start of their honeymoon, 20 November 1947.
Press Association Images.

Page 32
PA.6039461. The Duke of Edinburgh and his bride Princess Elizabeth walk through the woods at Broadlands, Romsey, on 23 November 1947 during the first days of their honeymoon. AP/Press Association Images.

Page 33
PA.800077. Prince Charles was christened Charles Philip Arthur George in a ceremony at Buckingham Palace on 15 December 1948. Looking on are George VI, Princess Elizabeth, Queen Elizabeth and the Duke of Edinburgh.
Press Association Images.

Page 34
PA.7172329. Princess Elizabeth, making an exception to the statement that she is to make no more public appearances until after the birth of her baby, leaves Westminster Abbey with Princess Margaret on 22 July 1948 after attending the wedding of Lord Derby and Isabel Milles-Lade. Press Association Images.

Page 35
PA.11141888. Princess Elizabeth and the Duke of Edinburgh in the grounds of Villa Guardamangia, Malta, on 23 November 1949, where the Princess is staying during her visit to the island.
AP/Press Association Images.

Page 36
PA.5377553. Prince Charles on his first birthday with his smiling mother, 14 November 1949. At 11 1/2 months the baby weighed 24 1/2 lbs, had six teeth and could walk a few steps by holding onto the sides of his playpen. Press Association Images.

PICTURE INDEX (continued)

Page 36
PA.2280554. Princess Elizabeth with her two children, one-month-old Princess Anne and Prince Charles, two months short of his second birthday, September 1951. Press Association Images.

Page 37
PA.1293111. The christening of Princess Anne, with her godparents, back row, left to right: Earl Mountbatten of Burma (her paternal granduncle); Princess Margarita of Hohenlohe-Langenburg (her paternal aunt); and the Hon. and Rev. Andrew Elphinstone (her cousin). Front row, from left: Princess Alice, Countess of Athlone; Princess Elizabeth holding Princess Anne, and Queen Elizabeth, Buckingham Palace, 21 October 1950. Press Association Images.

Page 38
PA.5370769. Princess Elizabeth and her two-year-old son Prince Charles watch from the wall of Clarence House as Queen Juliana and Prince Bernhard of the Netherlands ride in a procession to Guildhall, 22 November 1950. Press Association Images.

Page 39
PA.5335601. Princess Elizabeth at the Warner Theatre in London's Leicester Square for the premiere of the new British film *The Lady with the Lamp*, 22 September 1951. Press Association Images.

Page 40
PA.5370873. Princess Elizabeth arrives from Malta to be greeted by Prince Charles at London Airport, 24 April 1951. Press Association Images.

Page 41
PA.7178844. Officers and men aboard HMS *Tyne* salute Princess Elizabeth just before she disembarks after a visit to the Mediterranean fleet in Malta on 7 April 1951. Second from right is the Duke of Edinburgh. AP/Press Association Images.

Page 42
PA.7178850. Flanked by Vatican officials, Princess Elizabeth is escorted to the Clementine Hall for an audience with Pope Pius XII on 13 April 1951. AP/Press Association Images.

Page 43
PA.5883304. Princess Anne, in the arms of Princess Elizabeth, with the Duke of Edinburgh holding Prince Charles, in the grounds of Clarence House, their London residence, on 9 August 1951. Press Association Images.

Page 44
PA.2373663. Prince Charles, watched by King George VI, Princess Elizabeth, Prince Philip, Princess Margaret and Queen Elizabeth, sits on a sculpture of a deer in the grounds of Balmoral Castle, 16 August 1951. AP/Press Association Images.

Page 46
PA.11178195. Princess Elizabeth and the Duke of Edinburgh bid farewell to the people of St-Hyacinthe, Quebec, Canada, from the observation platform of the royal train on 8 November 1951. Press Association Images.

Page 47
PA.7259124 and PA.7259136. Princess Elizabeth and the Duke of Edinburgh enjoy a square dance at Government House in Ottawa, Ontario, on 11 October 1951. AP/Press Association Images.

Page 48
PA.7348389. King George VI, Queen Elizabeth and their younger daughter Princess Margaret cross the tarmac at London Airport to say farewell to Princess Elizabeth and her husband Prince Philip at the start of their 30,000-mile tour of Kenya, Ceylon, Australia and New Zealand, 31 January 1952. The King died six days later. AP/Press Association Images.

Page 49
PA.2685941. Princess Elizabeth and the Duke of Edinburgh pause on a bridge in the grounds of the Royal Lodge, Sagana, their wedding present from the people of Kenya, 2 February 1952. Press Association Images.

**CHAPTER 3:
THE NEW REIGN**

Page 50
PA.7348175. Queen Elizabeth II and the Duke of Edinburgh, centre with back to camera, are greeted on their arrival at London Airport, 7 February 1952. The royal couple cut short their official trip to Kenya and returned home following the death of King George VI. Prince Philip is talking to his uncle, Earl Mountbatten of Burma, left. AP/Press Association Images.

Page 52
PA.1152210. Queen Elizabeth II makes her first Christmas day broadcast to her people in the United Kingdom and around the world from Sandringham House, Norfolk, 25 December 1952. Press Association Images.

Page 52
PA.7310768. The Queen waves from the balcony at Buckingham Palace on 5 June 1952. The young monarch had just returned from the Trooping the Colour ceremony on Horse Guards Parade, the first of her reign. Press Association Images.

Page 53
Queen Elizabeth II, with the Duke of Edinburgh wearing the kilt, and their children, Princess Anne and Prince Charles at Balmoral Castle, 29 April 1953. Press Association Images.

Page 54
PA.1579905. The Queen alights from the Gold State Coach at Westminster Abbey and is met by her maids of honour before the Coronation, 2 June 1953. Press Association Images.

Page 55
PA.1579900. The Queen, sitting on St Edward's Chair, is crowned by the Archbishop of Canterbury in Westminster Abbey, 2 June 1953. Press Association Images.

Page 56
PA.11013343. Queen Elizabeth II, centre bottom, sits in St Edward's Chair shortly before she was lifted onto the throne by archbishops, bishops and other peers, 2 June 1953. AP/Press Association Images.

Page 57
PA.1093809. Queen Elizabeth II gives a wide smile for the crowd from the Gold State Coach as she leaves Westminster Abbey after her coronation, 2 June 1953. Press Association Images.

Page 57
PA.1131044. The Queen, with her children Charles and Anne on the balcony of Buckingham Palace, 2 June 1953. All look up as 168 fighter jets fly over the palace in the Royal Air Force salute to Her Majesty after the coronation ceremony at Westminster Abbey. Press Association Images.

Page 58
PA.11077246. The newly crowned Queen at Buckingham Palace with members of the royal family, 2 June 1953. Left to right: Princess Alexandra of Kent; Prince Michael of Kent; the Duchess of Kent; Princess Margaret; the Duke of Gloucester; Queen Elizabeth II; the Duke of Edinburgh; the Queen Mother; the Duke of Kent; Princess Mary, the Princess Royal; the Duchess of Gloucester; Prince William of Gloucester and Prince Richard of Gloucester. Press Association Images.

Page 60
PA.7277953. Flanked by Sir Alexander Hood, Governor of Bermuda, and by her husband, Queen Elizabeth II stands under a floral arch spelling out 'Long Live The Queen' and receives a speech of welcome at Hamilton, Bermuda, from Mayor E. R. Williamson, 24 November 1953. AP/Press Association Images.

Page 61
PA.6282185. Queen Elizabeth II is greeted by Sir Winston and Lady Churchill as she arrives for a dinner at No. 10 Downing Street, 5 April 1955. Press Association Images.

Page 62
PA.5623730, The Queen Mother, Princess Anne, the Queen and Princess Margaret at the Abergeldie royal sale of work, organised by the Queen Mother, on 20 August 1955. Press Association Images.

Page 63
PA.8683948. The Queen attends the Edinburgh Festival on 1 August 1956. AP/Press Association Images.

PA.10264952. Queen Elizabeth II and the Duke of Edinburgh attend a state dinner in Lagos, Nigeria, 1 February 1956. Press Association Images.

Page 64
PA.8670198. Queen Elizabeth II with Queen Elizabeth the Queen Mother and the Duke of Beaufort at the Badminton Horse Trials, 3 April 1957. AP/Press Association Images.

Page 65
PA.7270952. Queen Elizabeth II at her desk at Sandringham, Norfolk, on 25 December 1957, shortly after delivering her first televised Christmas Day broadcast. Pictures of her children, Charles and Anne, are on the desk. AP/Press Association Images.

Page 66
PA.7350846. Queen Elizabeth II chats with a group on nuns of Jersey, one of the Channel Islands, on 25 July 1957. Accompanied by Prince Philip, she made a one-day visit to Jersey and met people engaged in honorary service. AP/Press Association Images.

PA.7350841. Queen Elizabeth II arrives at London's Palace Theatre on 5 December 1956 for a performance of *Occupe-toi d'Amelie*, AP/Press Association Images.

Page 67
PA.7350845. The Queen meets actress Jayne Mansfield at London's Odeon Theatre on 4 November 1957. Miss Mansfield was one of many stars on hand when the Queen attended the annual royal film festival. AP/Press Association Images.

PICTURE INDEX (continued)

Page 68
PA.7588218. Queen Elizabeth II poses for a photograph at a White House state dinner in Washington, DC, 17 October 1957. AP/Press Association Images.

PA.7430648. The Queen, looking wistful, watches a B.O.A.C. Comet IV jet airliner carrying Prince Philip take off at London Airport on 20 January 1959, as the Duke left for New Delhi at the start of his world tour. With Her Majesty are Princess Margaret and Princess Anne. AP/Press Association Images.

Page 69
PA.7388782. Queen Elizabeth II and her host, Shah Mohammed Reza Pahlevi of Persia, as she arrives for dinner at the Persian Embassy in London on 6 May 1959. The Shah is on a state visit to England. AP/Press Association Images.

Page 70
PA.1131037. The Queen and Duke of Edinburgh with their children, Prince Charles and Princess Anne, on the East Terrace steps at Windsor Castle on 4 June 1959. Press Association Images.

Page 71
PA.1676323. The Queen and US President Dwight D. Eisenhower leaving the airstrip at St Hubert, Quebec, where Her Majesty greeted the President and his wife on their arrival in Canada, 29 June 1959. Press Association Images.

PA.7346755. Queen Elizabeth II arrives at Lord Beaverbrook Hotel in Fredericton, New Brunswick, on the last leg of her 45-day, 15,000-mile tour of Canada, 28 July 1959. AP/Press Association Images.

CHAPTER 4: THE 1960s

Page 72
PA.7270586. The royal family sit on blankets on the ground at Balmoral Castle in Scotland on 8 September 1960. Baby Prince Andrew, in the lap of his father, Prince Philip, reaches for a trinket presented by his mother, Queen Elizabeth II. Princess Anne and Prince Charles try to catch their brother's attention. AP/Press Association Images.

Page 73
PA.5178210. The Queen holds Prince Andrew during an outing at Balmoral, 8 September 1960. Press Association Images.

Page 74
PA.2888862. Queen Elizabeth II poses in the Green Drawing Room at Buckingham Palace for a study by Antony Buckley released to mark the forthcoming royal tour of India and Pakistan. The Queen and Prince Philip leave London for India on 20 January 1961. Campress/AP/Press Association Images.

Page 75
PA.2888859. Queen Elizabeth II addresses a gathering of more than a quarter of a million people at the Ramlila Grounds, a huge public meeting place outside the walls of Old Delhi, India, 28 January 1961. It was by far the largest audience ever directly addressed by the sovereign. AP/Press Association Images.

Page 76
PA.7454919. Queen Elizabeth II, well guarded atop the elephant on the left, watches native beaters drive through jungle overgrowth on a tiger hunt in Nepal, 2 March 1961. The Queen and Prince Philip were guests of King Mahendra on the hunt near Kathmandu. AP/Press Association Images.

Page 77
PA.7310950. Pope John XXIII and Queen Elizabeth II in the Clementine Hall at the Vatican on 5 May 1961, after the monarch's audience with the Pontiff. In the background is Prince Philip. AP/Press Association Images.

Page 78
PA.1362587. US President John F. Kennedy and his wife Jacqueline with Queen Elizabeth II and the Duke of Edinburgh at Buckingham Palace on 5 June 1961. The American couple were attending a dinner in their honour. Press Association Images.

Page 79
PA.7330187. Queen Elizabeth II smiles as she dances with Prime Minister Sir Milton Margai of Sierra Leone. The Queen, on a state visit to African countries, was at a ball at Fort Thornton in Freetown on 30 November 1961. AP/Press Association Images.

PA.7270970. Queen Elizabeth II wears a large feather in her hat at the Badminton Horse Trials in Gloucestershire on 14 April 1962. AP/Press Association Images.

Page 80
PA.7259448. Queen Elizabeth II and Prince Philip board an aircraft at London Airport on 31 January 1963 to start a two-month tour of Fiji, Australia and New Zealand. Their first stop was Vancouver, British Columbia. AP/Press Association Images.

Page 81
PA.1421551. HM The Queen rides side-saddle as she returns to Buckingham Palace after attending the Trooping the Colour ceremony on Horse Guards Parade, 8 June 1963.
Press Association Images.

Page 82
PA.7207753. Queen Elizabeth II with Prince Andrew and her fourth child Prince Edward on 12 June 1964. Edward was born on 10 March of that year.
AP/Press Association Images.

Page 83
PA.7270565. Queen Elizabeth II and the Duke of Edinburgh wave from the balcony of Buckingham Palace on 12 June 1965 after taking part in Trooping the Colour. With them are their two youngest children, Edward, left, and Andrew. AP/Press Association Images.

PA.8667391. Queen Elizabeth II wears a feathered hat at the Royal Maundy ceremony in Canterbury Cathedral on 15 April 1965. The monarch distributed Maundy coins, without current value, to 39 men and 39 women to mark her 39 years of age.
AP/Press Association Images.

Page 84
PA.7276976. Queen Elizabeth II with the Earl of Avon, who entertained the royal visitor at his house, Villa Nova, in Barbados, West Indies, on 15 February 1966. The Queen and Prince Philip are on a tour of the Caribbean.
AP/Press Association Images.

PA.7022161. The Queen and Prince Philip wave to the crowd from the balcony of Parliament House, Port of Spain, Trinidad, after the State Opening of Parliament, 8 February 1966.
AP/Press Association Images.

Page 85
PA.1161102. England captain Bobby Moore holds the Jules Rimet Trophy, collected from the Queen, after leading his team to a 4-2 victory over West Germany in an exciting World Cup Final that went to extra time at Wembley, 30 July 1966.
Press Association Images.

Page 86
PA.3422506. Queen Elizabeth II is seen during the State Opening of Parliament in London on 15 April 1966. AP/Press Association Images.

Page 87
10509482. The Queen views the destruction to the village of Aberfan on 29 September 1966 after a catastrophic collapse of a colliery spoil-tip that killed 116 children and 28 adults. Illustrated London News/Mary Evans Picture Library.

Page 88
PA.1409879. A slight bow from the Duke of Windsor as, with the Duchess of Windsor, he sees the Queen arrive at Marlborough House, London, on 7 June 1967 to unveil a plaque commemorating the centenary of the birth of his mother, Queen Mary (died 1953). Queen Mary lived at Marlborough House for 17 years.
Press Association Images.

PA.1126878. The Queen with King Faisal of Saudi Arabia when she and Prince Philip were the King's guests at a banquet in their honour at London's Dorchester Hotel, 16 May 1967. Press Association Images.

Page 89
PA.5183429. The Queen, Prince Charles, Prince Edward, Prince Andrew and Princess Anne listening to the Duke of Edinburgh on a bridge in the grounds of Frogmore, Home Park, Windsor, on 9 April 1968.
Press Association Images.

Page 90
PA.7556002. Queen Elizabeth II with Princess Anne, 17, at Benenden School in Kent, when she visited the school's 'Hobbies Day' on 20 July 1968. Three days later, the Princess became a 'Senior' – the school's term for an old girl. AP/Press Association Images.

Page 91
PA.7259522. Queen Elizabeth II, wearing the robes of the Order of St Michael and St George, leaves St Paul's Cathedral with Prince Philip on 21 July 1968 after attending the 150th anniversary service of the order.
AP/Press Association Images.

Page 92
PA.7430780. Members of the royal family leave St George's Chapel at Windsor on 25 December 1968 after the Christmas morning service.
AP/Press Association Images.

Page 93
PA.8694850. Queen Elizabeth II talks to Royal Canadian Mounted Police Staff-Sergeant Kave, mounted on Burmese, in the grounds of Windsor Castle, 28 April 1969.
AP/Press Association Images.

Page 94
PA.7206731. The Queen with Prince Charles, his five-year-old brother Prince Edward and a pet corgi at Windsor Castle on 20 June 1969.
AP/Press Association Images.

The Queen's Diamond Jubilee 215

PICTURE INDEX (continued)

Page 95
PA.1126103. The Queen places the coronet on Prince Charles's head during his investiture as Prince of Wales at Caernarfon Castle on 1 July 1969. Press Association Images.

CHAPTER 5: THE 1970s

Page 96
PA.1855948. Queen Elizabeth II and Prime Minister Edward Heath with American President Richard Nixon and his wife Pat at Chequers in Buckinghamshire on 3 October 1970. Press Association Images.

Page 97
PA.11085473. The Queen with the veiled Duchess of Windsor leaving St George's Chapel following the funeral service for the Duke of Windsor on 5 June 1972. Press Association Images.

Page 98
PA.4928856. Queen Elizabeth II and the Duke of Edinburgh pose for photographs at Balmoral on 1 September 1972 to mark their forthcoming Silver Wedding anniversary. Press Association Images.

Page 99
PA.1132238. The royal family at Buckingham Palace on 20 November 1972, the Queen and Prince Philip's Silver Wedding anniversary. Press Association Images.

Page 100
PA.10263193. The Queen, Princess Margaret, the Duke of Beaufort, Prince Edward and the Queen Mother watch the Badminton Horse Trials from a farm wagon, 21 April 1973. Press Association Images.

Page 100
PA.7424953. Queen Elizabeth II is in a happy mood during her visit to the international headquarters of the Boys' and Girls' Brigade in southwest London on 22 February 1973. AP/Press Association Images.

Page 101
PA.5210711. The Queen sits on a grassy bank at Virginia Water with her corgis to watch competitors, including Prince Philip, in the marathon section of the Royal Windsor Horse Show, 12 May 1973. Press Association Images.

Page 102
PA.3812250. Queen Elizabeth II enters the Sydney Opera House complex, Sydney, Australia, on 20 October 1973 to take part in the official opening ceremonies. AP/Press Association Images.

PA.7332623. The Queen enjoys a performance of aboriginal Canadian dancing at Mount McKay in Thunder Bay, Canada, 3 July 1973. Sitting with Her Majesty is Chief Frank Pelletier of the Fort William Indian Band. AP/Press Association Images.

Page 103
PA.1168901. The scene inside Westminster Abbey as Princess Anne weds Captain Mark Phillips on 14 November 1973. Press Association Images.

Page 104
PA.8640877. The Queen visits the Thomas Coram Foundation for Children in London on 12 February 1975. AP/Press Association Images.

Page 105
PA.9415303. The Queen during her visit to Silverwood Colliery near Rotherham on 30 July 1975. Press Association Images.

Page 105
PA.1518851. Thumbs in her pockets, the Queen, accompanied by her youngest son Prince Edward, strolls through crowds at the Badminton Horse Trials on 10 April 1976. Press Association Images.

Page 106
PA.5349939. The Duke of Edinburgh, Princess Anne, Mark Phillips, Prince Edward, the Queen, Prince Andrew and the Prince of Wales in Bromont, Canada, for the Olympic Games, 25 July 1976. Empics Entertainment.

PA.7376170. Queen Elizabeth II waves from the balcony of the White House on 7 July 1976 as she stands with President Gerald Ford and his wife Betty. AP/Press Association Images.

Page 107
PA.4928950. Queen Elizabeth II and the Duke of Edinburgh during their traditional summer break at Balmoral Castle, 26 September 1976. Press Association Images.

Page 108
PA.8219881. Queen Elizabeth II, wearing a cloak of brown kiwi feathers, with Maori warriors at Rugby Park, Gisborne, New Zealand, on 26 February 1977. Empics Entertainment.

Page 109
PA.1245768. Queen Elizabeth II enjoys a government reception at Parliament House, Canberra, on 8 March 1977 during her Silver Jubilee tour of Australia. Press Association Images.

PA.5183593. Queen Elizabeth II at work at her desk at Windsor Castle, 12 April 1977. Press Association Images.

Page 110
PA.8647315. The Queen attends a gala performance at the Royal Opera House, Covent Garden, on 30 May 1977 to mark her Silver Jubilee.
AP/Press Association Images.

PA.4306929. The Queen, Prince Philip and the Queen Mother with US President Jimmy Carter in the Blue Drawing Room at Buckingham Palace, where an official dinner was held, 7 May 1977.
Press Association Images.

Page 111
PA.1173094. The Gold State Coach at St Paul's Cathedral after arriving with the Queen and Duke of Edinburgh to attend a special service of thanksgiving for the Silver Jubilee, 7 June 1977.
Press Association Images.

Page 112
PA.1621223. Queen Elizabeth II accepts a posy of flowers from a well-wisher during her walkabout in the City of London after the Silver Jubilee service at St Paul's Cathedral, 7 June 1977.
Press Association Images.

Page 113
PA.5183624. Queen Elizabeth II and Prince Edward shield their ears at RAF Finningley, near Doncaster, during the Silver Jubilee Review of the Royal Air Force, 29 July 1977.
Press Association Images.

PA.600376. The Queen presents Britain's Virginia Wade with the Ladies' Singles trophy at the All-England Lawn Tennis Club, Wimbledon, London SW19, 1 July 1977. S&G and Barratts/Empics Sport.

Page 114
PA.7026880. Queen Elizabeth II, on her Silver Jubilee tour of the Caribbean, is greeted by Union Jack-carrying youngsters in Antigua, 29 October 1977.
Press Association Images.

PA.1381729. The Queen receives a posy from a young islander in fancy dress on Mustique, 30 October 1977. With her is Princess Margaret, who had a villa on the island. Press Association Images.

Page 115
PA.1326692. Queen Elizabeth II visits the flight deck of the supersonic Concorde during her journey home from Bridgetown, Barbados, after her Silver Jubilee tour of the West Indies, 2 November 1977.
Press Association Images.

Page 116
PA.1135144. Relatives and godparents of Princess Anne's 37-day-old son Master Peter Mark Andrew Phillips in the White Drawing Room at Buckingham Palace after his christening on 22 December 1977. Back row from left: Captain Hamish Lochore, the Duke of Edinburgh, Mrs Anne Phillips, Prince Charles, the Queen, Mr Peter Phillips, Captain Mark Phillips, the Queen Mother, Mrs Timothy Holderness-Roddam and Lady Cecil Cameron of Lochiel. Front row: Princess Alice, Countess of Athlone and Princess Anne holding her son.
Press Association Images.

Page 117
PA.1132200. Queen Elizabeth II with the Duke of Edinburgh, their children Prince Charles, Princess Anne, Prince Andrew and Prince Edward, and their first grandchild, Peter Phillips, at Balmoral, 1 September 1979. Press Association Images.

Page 118
PA.8630134. Queen Elizabeth II is escorted by King Khalid of Saudi Arabia, far right, after her arrival at Riyadh Airport on 17 February 1979.
Press Association Images.

Page 119
PA.1128927. Prince Charles reads the lesson during Earl Mountbatten of Burma's funeral service in Westminster Abbey, 5 September 1979.
Press Association Images.

CHAPTER 6: THE 1980s

Page 120
PA.11662166. The Queen and members of the royal family on the steps of St Paul's Cathedral after the service of thanksgiving in honour of the Queen Mother's 80th birthday, 15 July 1980. With them is Sir Peter Gadsden, Lord Mayor of London.
Press Association Images.

Page 121
PA.11662224. The Queen Mother leaves the service of thanksgiving marking her forthcoming 80th birthday, 15 July 1980. Behind her is the Prince of Wales and the Master of Horse, the Earl of Westmoreland.
Press Association Images.

Page 122
PA.2892318. Queen Elizabeth II eats with her hands in the desert with King Hassan during her state visit to Morocco, 27 October 1980.
Empics Entertainment.

Page 123
PA.1129436. The Queen with Prince Charles and his fiancée, Lady Diana Spencer, at Buckingham Palace after a Privy Council meeting on 27 March 1981. Press Association Images.

The Queen's Diamond Jubilee 217

PICTURE INDEX (continued)

Page 124
PA.1813331. An official group photograph in the Throne Room at Buckingham Palace after the wedding of the Prince and Princess of Wales on 29 July 1981. Amongst the guests pictured are the Queen, the Queen Mother, the Duke of Edinburgh, Princess Anne, Princess Margaret, Earl Spencer and Ruth, Lady Fermoy, Diana's grandmother.
Press Association Images.

Page 125
PA.1532407. Corgi puppies are carried on to an aircraft as the Queen arrives at London's Heathrow Airport to board her flight to Aberdeen and the start of her annual holiday at Balmoral, 5 August 1981.
Press Association Images.

PA.2318808. Queen Elizabeth II bids farewell to Pope John Paul II at Buckingham Palace on 28 May 1982.
Press Association Images.

Page 126
PA.7508156. Queen Elizabeth II and Colonel Hugh Brassey on the terrace overlooking the garden of Buckingham Palace before a march-past of the Yeomen of the Guard, her personal bodyguard, on 23 June 1982.
AP/Press Association Images.

PA.4930518. President Reagan is entertained by the Queen at a banquet in St George's Hall, Windsor Castle, on 8 June 1982.
Press Association Images.

Page 127
PA.1134727. The royal family at Buckingham Palace on 4 August 1982 for Prince William's christening. It was also the Queen Mother's 82nd birthday. Press Association Images.

Page 128
PA.7206724. Queen Elizabeth II rocks with mirth after her hand stuck to that of shot-putter Geoff Capes at the Braemar Gathering on 5 September 1982, when he won the caber tossing. He warned the Queen that he had been unable to wash off the resin, used to improve grip, from his hands, but she shook hands with him anyway. AP/Press Association Images.

PA.1413833. The Queen, Prince Andrew, the Duke of Edinburgh and Princess Anne on board the aircraft carrier HMS *Invincible* after the Prince's return from the Falkland Islands, 17 September 1982.
Press Association Images.

Page 129
PA.1254759. Queen Elizabeth II and the Duke of Edinburgh are carried shoulder high in canoes during their visit to Tuvalu in the South Sea Islands, 26 October 1982.
Press Association Images.

PA.1254756. The Queen takes photographs during their visit to the South Sea island of Tuvalu, 26 October 1982. Press Association Images.

Page 130
PA.4930319. The Queen and Prince Philip with President Ronald Reagan and his wife Nancy at a state dinner at the M. H. de Young Museum in San Francisco's Golden Gate Park on 3 March 1983. AP/Press Association Images.

PA.1027623. Mother Teresa receives the insignia of the Order of Merit from the Queen in New Delhi, India, on 1 November 1983.
Press Association Images.

Page 131
PA.1750678. Queen Elizabeth II at the Martyr's Memorial in Amman on 27 March 1984 during her state visit to Jordan. Press Association Images.

Page 131
PA.7270978. The Queen smiles as she tours the Royal Bath and West Show at Shepton Mallet, Somerset, 31 May 1985. AP/Press Association Images.

Page 132
PA.8657760. Queen Elizabeth II leaves the Royal Chapel in Windsor Great Park after a service on the eve of her 60th birthday, 20 April 1986.
AP/Press Association Images.

The Queen collects flowers during a walkabout before a gala performance at the Royal Opera House, Covent Garden, to mark her 60th birthday, 21 April 1986. Joe Little.

Page 133
PA.1518848. A distressing moment for the Queen and Princess Margaret inside the fire-damaged south wing of the 16th-century Hampton Court Palace, 31 March 1986. Press Association Images.

PA.7348880. Queen Elizabeth II and Prince Philip arrive at Royal Ascot in a landau on 18 June 1986.
AP/Press Association Images.

Page 134
PA.1168857. The Duke and Duchess of York on the balcony of Buckingham Palace after their wedding on 23 July 1986. Press Association Images.

Page 135
PA.1409091. Queen Elizabeth II and the Duke of Edinburgh on the Great Wall of China on the third day of their state visit to the country, 14 October 1986. Press Association Images.

PA.7332618. The Queen inspects the famous Terracotta Warriors in Xian, China, 16 October 1986.
AP/Press Association Images.

Page 136
PA.7317203. Queen Elizabeth II strokes Tourmalay, a two-year-old piebald, during a visit to a stud farm in Normandy, France, on 23 May 1987. AP/Press Association Images.

Page 137
PA.3386378. The Queen and the Princess of Wales at Clarence House on 4 August 1987 for the Queen Mother's 87th birthday celebrations. AP/Press Association Images.

PA.8694793. Queen Elizabeth II attends a thanksgiving service at St Paul's Church in London on 10 February 1988. AP/Press Association Images.

Page 138
PA.7424367. The Queen entertains the Soviet leader Mikhail Gorbachev at Windsor Castle on 7 April 1989. AP/Press Association Images.

Page 139
PA.7424610. Queen Elizabeth II shows her excitement as the American-bred favourite Hashwan, ridden by Willie Carson, crossed the line to win the 210th Derby at Epsom racecourse, 7 June 1989. AP/Press Association Images.

Page 140
PA.2373503. Queen Elizabeth II presents former US President Ronald Reagan with the insignia of an Honorary Knight Grand Cross of the Most Honourable Order of the Bath after a luncheon at Buckingham Palace on 14 June 1989. AP/Press Association Images.

Page 141
PA.7450100. Queen Elizabeth II walks with the King of Malaysia during welcoming ceremonies in Kuala Lumpur on 14 October 1989. The Queen is on a state visit and will open the 46-nation Commonwealth Summit. AP/Press Association Images.

PA.10026616. The Queen attends the Royal Variety Performance at the London Palladium, Argyll Street, London W1, on 21 November 1989. Empics Entertainment.

CHAPTER 7: THE 1990s

Page 142
PA.1518855. The Queen Mother celebrates her 90th birthday at Clarence House, 4 August 1990. With her are Prince Philip, Peter Phillips, Viscount Linley, the Princess Royal, Lady Sarah Armstrong-Jones, the Queen, Prince Edward, the Prince and Princess of Wales and Princess Margaret. Press Association Images.

Page 144
The Queen and President Lech Walesa of Poland travel in the 1902 State Landau to Windsor Castle at the start of his state visit to Britain, 23 April 1991. Joe Little.

The Queen attends Matins at the church of St Mary Magdalene on the Sandringham estate, 4 August 1991. Joe Little.

Page 145
PA.7360689. Queen Elizabeth II peers through microphones while giving a speech on the South Lawn of the White House on 14 May 1991. President George Bush looks on. AP/Press Association Images.

Page 145
PA.7361244. President and Mrs Bush with Queen Elizabeth II and Prince Philip upon arrival at a dinner hosted by the Queen at the British Embassy in Washington on 16 May 1991. AP/Press Association Images.

Page 146
PA.1290542. Four generations of the royal family – the Queen, the Prince of Wales, the Queen Mother, the Princess of Wales and Lady Gabriella Windsor, daughter of Prince Michael of Kent – on the balcony of Buckingham Palace after Trooping the Colour, 13 June 1992. Press Association Images.

The Queen with a traditional nosegay after the Royal Maundy service in Chester Cathedral on 16 April 1992. Joe Little.

Page 147
PA.8040582. The fire continues to rage at Windsor Castle on 20 November 1992. Press Association Images.

PA.1300943. The Queen inspects the ruins of Windsor Castle with a senior fire officer, 21 November 1992. Press Association Images.

Page 148
PA.1414639. The Queen shelters under an umbrella during the Royal Air Force's 75th anniversary celebration at RAF Marham, Norfolk, 1 April 1993. Bad weather caused the cancellation of the fly-past and cut proceedings short. Press Association Images.

Page 149
PA.1380636. The Queen and President Boris Yeltsin join in a toast during a banquet at the Kremlin in Moscow at the end of the first full day of her state visit to Russia, 18 October 1994. Press Association Images.

The Queen's Diamond Jubilee 219

PICTURE INDEX (continued)

Page 150
PA.1380659. The Queen, the Queen Mother and Princess Margaret watch vintage planes fly over Buckingham Palace as part of the commemorations for the 50th anniversary of VE-Day, 8 May 1995. Press Association Images.

Page 151
PA.1022887. The Queen holds flowers after leaving a church service at Sandringham on her 70th birthday, 21 April 1996. Press Association Images.

PA.2894334. The Queen and the King of Thailand toast each other at a state banquet in the Chakri Palace Throne Hall in Bangkok, 28 October 1996. Press Association Images.

Page 152
PA.1038563. Prince William with his family and godparents in the White Drawing Room at Windsor Castle after his confirmation at St George's Chapel on 9 March 1997. Front, left to right: Prince Harry, Diana, Princess of Wales, Prince William, the Prince of Wales and the Queen. Back row: King Constantine of Greece, Lady Susan Hussey, Princess Alexandra, the Duchess of Westminster and Lord Romsey. Press Association Images.

Page 153
PA.1057729. The Queen and the Duke of Edinburgh view the floral tributes to Diana, Princess of Wales at Buckingham Palace on 5 September 1997. Press Association Images.

Page 154
PA.1066696. The Queen and the Duke of Edinburgh are joined by members of their family at Westminster Abbey on 20 November 1997 for a service to celebrate their Golden Wedding anniversary. Press Association Images.

Page 155
PA.1096498. Queen Elizabeth II and Japanese Emperor Akihito of Japan, his wife Empress Michiko, the Duke of Edinburgh and Queen Elizabeth the Queen Mother pause for photographs before a state banquet at Buckingham Palace on 26 May 1998.
Press Association Images.

Page 156
PA.1143493. The Prince of Wales with his mother at Buckingham Palace for a reception in his honour on the eve of his 50th birthday, 13 November 1998. Press Association Images.

Page 157
PA.1199798. The Earl and Countess of Wessex, with the Queen and Mr Christopher Rhys-Jones, leave St George's Chapel, Windsor Castle, following their wedding, 19 June 1999. Press Association Images.

PA.1199788. The Queen is clearly enjoying the wedding of her youngest son, Prince Edward, to Sophie Rhys-Jones, 19 June 1999. Press Association Images.

Page 158
PA.1204242. Queen Elizabeth II opens the Scottish Parliament in Edinburgh, 1 July 1999. Press Association Images.

PA.1205931. The Queen is introduced to Quorn the guide dog during a garden party at the Palace of Holyroodhouse in Edinburgh, 6 July 1999.
Press Association Images.

Page 159
PA.1206156. The Queen joins Mrs Susan McCarron and her 10-year-old son James for tea in their home in the Castlemilk area of Glasgow, 7 July 1999. Press Association Images.

Page 160
PA.1249176. Irish President Mary McAleese attends a private lunch in her honour at Buckingham Palace, 2 December 1999. The meeting of the two heads of state took on added significance coming as it did on Devolution Day in Northern Ireland. Press Association Images.

Page 161
PA.1257036. The Queen joins Prime Minister Tony Blair and wife Cherie singing *Auld Lang Syne* during the celebrations to welcome in the new year at the Millennium Dome in Greenwich, 31 December 1999. Press Association Images.

CHAPTER 8: THE 2000s

Page 162
PA.1329310. Princess Margaret, Queen Elizabeth the Queen Mother and Queen Elizabeth II on the balcony of Buckingham Palace on 4 August 2000 during the celebration for the Queen Mother's 100th birthday. Press Association Images.

Page 164
PA.1405358. Queen Elizabeth II after recording her Commonwealth Day message at Buckingham Palace, 20 February 2001. Press Association Images.

Page 165
PA.1560382. The Queen and the Prince of Wales walk behind Queen Elizabeth the Queen Mother's coffin following her funeral at Westminster Abbey on 9 April 2002. Press Association Images.

Page 166
PA.1581200. Fireworks burst over Buckingham Palace after Queen Elizabeth II lit a beacon to commemorate her Golden Jubilee, 3 June 2002. Earlier, some 12,000 people had watched *Party at the Palace* – the second concert to be held in the garden in three days – while a crowd estimated at one million gathered outside to enjoy the music. Press Association Images.

Page 167
PA.1581289. Queen Elizabeth II waves to the crowd as she rides in the Gold State Coach from Buckingham Palace to St Paul's Cathedral for a service of thanksgiving to celebrate her Golden Jubilee, 4 June 2002. Press Association Images.

Page 168
PA.1749737. Queen Elizabeth II, her oldest son, the Prince of Wales, and his oldest son, Prince William, pose for a photograph at Clarence House on 2 June 2003 before a dinner to mark the 50th anniversary of her coronation. Press Association Images.

Page 169
PA.1769771. The Queen inspects a model depicting the fire that destroyed St Paul's Church in Deptford, which was restored by the Historic Churches Preservation Trust, 17 July 2003. Press Association Images.

PA.1915209. Queen Elizabeth II peers round a corner during a visit to the Royal Albert Hall in London to mark the end of an eight-year restoration programme. 30 March 2004. Press Association Images.

Page 170
PA.2324971. The Prince of Wales and his bride the Duchess of Cornwall with their families in the White Drawing Room at Windsor Castle, 9 April 2005. Back row, left to right: Prince Harry, Prince William, Tom and Laura Parker Bowles. Front row: the Duke of Edinburgh, the Queen and Camilla's father, Major Bruce Shand. Hugo Burnand/Press Association Images.

Page 171
PA.4586103. Queen Elizabeth II in the Regency Room at Buckingham Palace on 20 April 2006 as she looks at some of the cards sent to her for her 80th birthday. Press Association Images.

PA.3431811. The Queen passes a gift of a Union Jack baseball cap to her equerry during a walkabout in Windsor on her 80th birthday, 21 April 2006. Press Association Images.

Page 172
PA.4636570. The Queen smiles as she is greeted by astronauts aboard the International Space Station, via video conference, during her visit to NASA's Goddard Flight Center in Greenbelt, Maryland, on 8 May 2007. AP/Press Association Images.

PA.4632392. Queen Elizabeth II and US President George W. Bush deliver speeches at the White House in Washington DC on 7 May 2007. Press Association Images.

Page 173
PA.5355538. Queen Elizabeth II and the Duke of Edinburgh are joined by their family for a dinner hosted by the Prince of Wales and the Duchess of Cornwall at Clarence House to mark their forthcoming Diamond Wedding anniversary, 18 November 2007. Tim Graham/Press Association Images.

Page 173
PA.5354188. The Queen and Prince Philip at Broadlands in Hampshire in the autumn of 2007. They began their honeymoon there in November 1947. Press Association Images.

Page 174
PA.5957048. Queen Elizabeth II waves off her eldest grandson Peter Phillips and his new wife Autumn outside St George's Chapel, Windsor Castle, after their wedding on 17 May 2008. Press Association Images.

Page 175
PA.6922359. Queen Elizabeth II arrives for the unveiling of a statue of Queen Elizabeth the Queen Mother in The Mall in central London, 24 February 2009. Press Association Images.

Page 176
PA.7079491. Queen Elizabeth II and delegates of the G20 London summit pose for a group photograph in the Throne Room at Buckingham Palace, 1 April 2009. Press Association Images.

PA.7085494. Michelle Obama, wife of the US President Barack Obama, chats with the Queen at the reception at Buckingham Palace on 1 April 2009. AP/Press Association Images.

Page 177
PA.7437843. Queen Elizabeth II smiles at the Duke of Edinburgh during the annual Trooping the Colour parade on Horse Guards Parade on 13 June 2009. Press Association Images.

Page 178
PA.8071475. Queen Elizabeth II in the grounds of the President of Trinidad's official residence in Port of Spain before joining guests at a state dinner, 26 November 2009. Press Association Images.

PICTURE INDEX (continued)

Page 178
PA.8003526. The Queen walks along Northumberland Street in Newcastle during her visit to Tyne and Wear on 6 November 2009. Press Association Images.

Page 179
PA.8108151. Queen Elizabeth II meets American singer Lady Gaga backstage at the Royal Variety Performance in Blackpool on 7 December 2009. Press Association Images.

PA.8141432. The Queen waits for her First Capital Connect train to depart from King's Cross Station in London, from where she travelled by scheduled service to King's Lynn in Norfolk on 17 December 2009. She was then driven to Sandringham to spend Christmas with her family. Press Association Images.

CHAPTER 9: THE PRESENT DAY

Page 180
PA.8757106. Queen Elizabeth II is cheered by school children waving flags during a visit to Caernarfon Castle in north Wales on 27 April 2010. Press Association Images.

Page 182
PA.8619869. The Queen gives a reception at Windsor Castle for the Bloomsbury Qatar Foundation Publishing Project, 6 April 2010. Press Association Images.

Page 183
PA.8708292. Tactician and jockey Hayley Turner with owner Queen Elizabeth II after a victory at Newbury racecourse in Berkshire on 17 April 2010. Press Association Images.

Page 184
PA.9005977. Queen Elizabeth II and the Duke of Edinburgh return to Buckingham Palace in Queen Victoria's ivory mounted phaeton following the Trooping the Colour ceremony on Horse Guards Parade on 12 June 2010. Press Association Images.

PA.8845428. The Queen relaxes at the Royal Windsor Horse Show in the grounds of Windsor Castle, 14 May 2010. Press Association Images.

Page 185
PA.9117928. Queen Elizabeth II with Canadian Prime Minster Stephen Harper after she unveiled the design for a Diamond Jubilee stained glass window depicting herself and Queen Victoria at Government House in Ottawa, Canada, 30 June 2010. Press Association Images.

Page 186
PA.9137146. The Queen waits to greet guests at the Royal York Hotel in Toronto, where the Canadian government hosted a dinner in her honour on 5 July 2010. Maple leaves are incorporated into the design of her evening dress. Press Association Images.

PA.9137150. Queen Elizabeth II addresses guests at the Royal York Hotel dinner in Toronto on 5 July 2010. Press Association Images.

Page 187
PA.9147957. Queen Elizabeth II greets the crowd gathered outside Queen's Park in Toronto on 6 July 2010 as she ends her nine-day visit to Canada, before flying to New York to address the United Nations. Canadian Press/Press Association Images.

Page 188
PA.9474675. The Duke of Edinburgh looks on as Queen Elizabeth II and Pope Benedict XVI exchange gifts during an audience in the Morning Drawing Room at the Palace of Holyroodhouse in Edinburgh, 16 September 2010. Press Association Images.

Page 189
PA.9775814. Queen Elizabeth II is dressed in black for the Remembrance Sunday ceremony at the Cenotaph in Whitehall, central London, 14 November 2010. Press Association Images.

Page 190
PA.9840114. The Queen and the Sultan of Oman, His Majesty Sultan Qaboos bin Said, watch an equestrian event and horse racing at the Royal Horse Racing Club in Seeb, Oman, on 27 November 2010. Press Association Images.

Page 191
PA.10469214. Prince William shows the Queen the hangar where the Sea King Helicopter he flies during his training as a search and rescue pilot is kept during her visit to RAF Valley in Anglesey, north Wales, on 1 April 2011. Press Association Images.

Page 192
PA.10620531. The new Duke and Duchess of Cambridge on the balcony of Buckingham Palace following their wedding at Westminster Abbey on 29 April 2011. With them are the Queen, the Prince of Wales, the Duchess of Cornwall and Michael Middleton, and the younger wedding attendants. Press Association Images.

Page 193
PA.10619474. The Queen and Prince Philip attend the wedding of Prince William and Catherine Middleton at Westminster Abbey on 29 April 2011. Press Association Images.

Page 194
PA.10755689. Queen Elizabeth II with Irish President Mary McAleese after arriving at Áras an Uachtaráin in Phoenix Park, Dublin, on 17 May 2011. Their spouses Dr Martin McAleese and the Duke of Edinburgh look on. Press Association Images.

Page 195
PA.10769391. Queen Elizabeth II delivers her speech watched by Irish President Mary McAleese before a state dinner in St Patrick's Hall at Dublin Castle on the second day of her state visit to Ireland, 18 May 2011. Press Association Images.

Page 196
PA.10818592. The Queen and the Duke of Edinburgh with US President Barack Obama and his wife Michelle in the Music Room at Buckingham Palace on 24 May 2011 before a state banquet as part of the President's three-day state visit to the UK. Press Association Images.

Page 197
PA.10952984. Queen Elizabeth II and the Duke of Edinburgh arrive at St George's Chapel on 12 June 2011 for a service to mark his 90th birthday. Press Association Images.

Page 198
PA.11247863. The Queen talks with the Duchess of Cambridge at Buckingham Palace on 22 July 2011 as they view the wedding dress Catherine wore three months earlier before it goes on public display. Press Association Images.

Page 199
PA.11307942. Zara Phillips and Mike Tindall in Holyrood Abbey, Palace of Holyroodhouse, after their wedding on 30 July 2011. Robert Shack/Press Association Images.

PA.11305840. Queen Elizabeth II arrives at Canongate Kirk on 30 July 2011 for the wedding of her granddaughter Zara Phillips to Mike Tindall. Press Association Images.

CHAPTER 10: SIXTY GLORIOUS YEARS

Page 200
RCIN 400211. *'God Save The Queen': Queen Victoria arriving at St Paul's Cathedral on the occasion of the Diamond Jubilee Service, 22 June 1897*, by John Charlton. The Royal Collection © 2011, Her Majesty Queen Elizabeth II.

Page 202
RCIN 920871. *The Diamond Jubilee: the Queen entering St George's Chapel, Windsor, for the Thanksgiving Service, 20 June 1897*, by William Small. The Royal Collection © 2011, Her Majesty Queen Elizabeth II.

Page 203
105057181. Queen Victoria sits in her carriage outside St Paul's Cathedral on 22 June 1897. Mary Evans Picture Library.

Page 204
RCIN 920879. *The Diamond Jubilee: the Queen at St Paul's Cathedral, 22 June 1897*, by John Gulich. The Royal Collection © 2011, Her Majesty Queen Elizabeth II.

Page 206
The obverse and reverse of Queen Victoria's Diamond Jubilee Gold Medal. Private Collection.

Page 207
RCIN 2105789. A portrait of Queen Victoria by Gustav Mullins as she appeared on the day of her Diamond Jubilee celebrations, signed by the monarch and dated June 22 1897. The Royal Collection © 2011, Her Majesty Queen Elizabeth II.

Page 208
RCIN 405286. *The Queen's Garden Party* [at Buckingham Palace], *28 June 1897*, by Laurits Regner Tuxen. The Royal Collection © 2011, Her Majesty Queen Elizabeth II.

The Queen's Diamond Jubilee

Acknowledgments

I would like to thank the contributors – Robert Golden, Lucinda Gosling, Coryne Hall, Ian Lloyd, Ingrid Seward and Christopher Warwick – for their diligence and encouragement along the way.

I am also indebted to Darren Reeve and Annette Prosser, who were generous with their time and helped this book take shape.

Sarah Hill at Press Association Images and Katie Holyoak at the Royal Collection Picture Library must also be thanked for the assistance they so willingly provided.

Joe Little
Managing Editor, *Majesty* magazine

London, October 2011